Movement
Improvisation

COPY 1

DATE DUE			

VANCOUVER PUBLIC SCHOOLS
605 North Devine Road
Vancouver, WA 98661

Library of Congress Cataloging-in-Publication Data

Schneer, Georgette.
  Movement improvisation : in the words of a teacher and her
students / Georgette Schneer, 1994.
     p.   cm.
  ISBN 0-87322-530-9
  1. Improvisation in dance--Study and teaching.   I. Title.
GV1781.2.S36   1994
792.8--dc20   93-44419
                                                              CIP

ISBN: 0-87322-530-9

Acquisitions Editor: Judy Patterson Wright, PhD; **Developmental Editor:** Holly
Gilly; **Assistant Editors:** Sally Bayless, Jacqueline Blakley, Anna Curry, Julie
Lancaster, Dawn Roselund, and Matt Scholz; **Copyeditor:** Nancy Garrett; **Proof-
reader:** Kathy Bennett; **Indexer:** Judith B. Alter; **Typesetter:** Julie Overholt;
Text Designer: Jody Boles; **Layout Artist:** Tara Welsch; **Cover Designer:** Jack
Davis; **Illustrator:** Rochelle Robkin; **Printer:** United Graphics

Printed in the United States of America   10 9 8 7 6 5 4 3 2 1

Human Kinetics books are available at special discounts for bulk purchase.
Special editions or book excerpts can also be created to specification. For details,
contact the Special Sales Manager at Human Kinetics.

Human Kinetics
P.O. Box 5076, Champaign, IL 61825-5076
1-800-747-4457

Canada: Human Kinetics, Box 24040,
Windsor, ON N8Y 4Y9
1-800-465-7301 (in Canada only)

Europe: Human Kinetics, P.O. Box IW14,
Leeds LS16 6TR, England
(44) 532 781708

Australia: Human Kinetics, Unit 5, 32 Raglan Avenue,
Edwardstown 5039, South Australia
(08) 371 3755

New Zealand: Human Kinetics, P.O. Box 105-231, Auckland 1
(09) 309 2259

Contents

Foreword

"If you write your book, I will use it for my graduate students in dance education classes!" I said this repeatedly to my friend and mentor, Georgette Schneer. She would laugh her musical, effervescent laugh and tell me, "I am not a writer, I'm an improvisation teacher."

"But my students and I need it," I would reply. I won. *Movement Improvisation: In the Words of a Teacher and Her Students* came about because many knowledgeable people encouraged Georgette to write a book. They agreed that what she teaches and how she teaches it are treasures too valuable and life-giving to keep to herself and her students. With this book Georgette extends her teaching of improvisation to countless students and teachers who can share her sparkling, witty, and engaging wealth of ideas and experience and can hear directly from students what they learned in Georgette's classes.

Georgette Schneer was a childhood pupil of the legendary Bird Larson, who taught creative dance at New York's Neighborhood Playhouse when modern dance was emerging from its role in pageants to become an autonomous art form. She also studied with Irma Duncan. Georgette became a scholarship student of Doris Humphrey and then a member of her understudy group. She received a New Dance Group award to study Wigman technique with Fe Alf, and her performing career included dancing under Anna Sokolow, Lily Mehlman, and Benjamin Zemach.

In addition to performing, Georgette participated in the formative years of the New Dance Group in New York, the famous cooperative dance studio for teachers of many kinds of dance and numerous students. As director and choreographer for the Harlem Dance and Theatre Company she involved Lorraine Hansberry and Asadata Dafora, dean of African dancers in the United States. To this impressive background Georgette brings her unique flowing creativity, a buoyant attitude toward life, and brilliant insight into students' movement needs. She has been teaching improvisation for more than 40 years.

Georgette's vibrant writing style enables readers to envision themselves in class with this master teacher. And unique among movement books, Georgette weaves into her text emotionally moving transcripts of conversations with students, quotations that reveal the inherent values that Georgette's teaching embodies. For years she has been audiotaping these conversations, and now we benefit from her intuitive foresight to collect these thoughtfully honest responses to the experience of improvisation. One of her former students recently reflected on Georgette's classes: Human beings come first; her primary focus is on human beings and their movements. No hierarchical teacher–student relationship exists in her classes; her students teach her and each other. And trust is central: in oneself, in each classmate, and in Georgette. *Movement Improvisation* radiates these same values.

Being welcome is the first impression readers will experience in beginning this book. The second impression is of freedom; students are free to be themselves in these improvisation classes. Georgette answers the question students commonly ask: When I improvise should my movement be technically correct, 'dancey,' or pretty? Her response is to move from within; start from the heart. The third special element of this book is abundance; Georgette enables readers to see how abundant are source-ideas for improvising. She calls these source-ideas, or movement stimuli, "themes" and includes more than 160 with numerous variations. In describing the many unpredictable ways students have developed these themes, Georgette encourages teachers to open their minds and eyes to improvisers' unique responses.

Georgette Schneer understands improvisation as a springboard to art and vital preparation for choreographing dances. To implement her view that movement in the moment should be recognized as an enriching creative experience, she espouses giving quality attention to students as they improvise before the entire group. Here Georgette answers another question teachers frequently ask: Should students show their improvisations? If so, how should the others respond? Georgette recommends that class members watch with supportive nonverbal appreciation as each improviser gains freedom, confidence, and depth in creative movement work. This silent sharing adds to everyone's knowledge and appreciation of each person's humanity.

Throughout the book Georgette answers many other questions that movement leaders have about teaching improvisation. Creativity is the key to each of her answers. As a facilitator Georgette does not show students what to do; instead she provides verbal guidance, continual encouragement, and specific positive praise. Leaders of movement improvisation need not be proficient facilitators to conduct these sessions; they need only to see carefully and guide effectively. (It does help if they have had some experience in improvising because they will more easily recognize when students need further guidance.) And without being shown or told how to respond to a particular theme, students discover their own way of interpreting it; thus, their unique, spontaneous way is the "right" way.

The central focus of *Movement Improvisation* is students—the individual and the group: their self-confidence, self-knowledge, and self-concept within the group. Georgette Schneer is proudest of the rich interaction that her improvisation classes provide. They enable human beings to grow and flourish and to celebrate their individuality, their dynamic power, and their creativity in motion. This special emphasis on the group helps teachers master the challenge of creating a cohesive whole out of a collection of individuals. Among her colleagues, Georgette is known for her ability to bring a group of improvisors to feeling comfortably unified. Her vision encompasses the broadest range of students: Anyone who can move has the potential to enjoy and learn from improvisation. This lively and living book will enrich your teaching, your art, and your spirit as you enjoy the wit and wisdom of Georgette Schneer and the freewheeling, imaginative illustrations of artist and art teacher Rochelle Robkin.

Judith B. Alter, EdD

Preface

This book explores improvised movement—also called creative movement, or expressive movement—and its spontaneity, its spur-of-the moment character. This unplanned, unrehearsed, and unfeigned movement represents the sum of our everyday actions as we respond to whatever wells up within us: our gestures, facial expressions, and movements of the head, extremities, and torso, either by themselves or together. Movement improvisation encompasses whatever it is we do when we are "feelingful." In *Movement Improvisation* I take a wide-lens view of the myriad human movements. I honor silent communication and believe that we each possess a treasure of improvising potential. Often left untapped, were these skills honed they would allow each of us to become ever more eloquent. By using the varied means in this book, including props and themes to increase awareness and cooperation and stimuli to arouse imagery, fantasy, and emotion, we can recapture our free and physical expressiveness.

I include a step-by-step description of how to conduct class segments, with examples from classes where these methods have been used. Throughout, I intentionally emphasize teaching to the positive, which I mean to be inspirational. Part I defines improvisation and explains that anyone can be an artist and that creativity can be taught. Part II describes the benefits of movement improvisation to an individual and to a group, class procedure, and how to stimulate and develop group activity. Part III explains five principles of movement improvisation and how to create physical and emotional safety. I also discuss freedom, working with people who are shy and others who show off, and how to nurture adult beginners. Part IV contains themes: what they are, how to make them, and how to build on tiny movement responses. You will find tips on what to look for, stimulate, and reinforce in the improvisations.

I am especially proud of three features of *Movement Improvisation*: the rich and varied themes section, the quotations, and the nontechnical language, which I hope will help facilitators and students who do not work exclusively in the performing arts. The themes section outlines specific motivations for movement; gives creative experiences with such concepts as rhythm, tempo, line, and dynamics; and relates movement to place and space and to shape and form. The section charts 135 themes that help release artistic, emotional, social, technical, and imaginative expression for novice and experienced improvisers, for solo, and for groups of any number. Almost 30 more special themes follow—for holidays and seasons, for integrating the individual into the group, and for welding a group together. Some themes might appropriately be accompanied by self-produced sound or percussion (see Part II). I also offer a guide to help you originate themes.

You will find quotations throughout the book, denoted by three dancing figures (my studio logo). These quotations, from audiotapes of student interviews over the past 15 years, discuss personal and group experiences, body images, inhibitions, risks, discoveries, development, and growth. We can all learn from and identify with many of these candid, subtle, and painful revelations. I read these quotes with joy, sadness, laughter, and especially with humility. The book's title, *Movement Improvisation: In the Words of a Teacher and Her Students*, in fact, was stimulated by these illuminating quotations. My students include people from all walks of life and these italicized quotes reveal the diversity of their improvisation experiences in their own unedited words.

I share with you the know-how that comes from my study with my students, whatever your movement-oriented field, discipline, or program. These ideas and themes will enhance nonverbal relations even for readers without formal movement training. Certainly, parents of preschoolers will find valuable hints for educational play and personality development.

In *dance and theater*, this book will aid teachers and students at all levels throughout the spectrum of performance, choreography, aesthetics, and recreation. Creative movement can be practiced also in *dance therapy* one-to-one or in hospitals and institutions where the nonverbal can substitute for what cannot be expressed in words and help gain access to the verbal.

Formal education has the difficult mission of addressing all our varied cultures merged within a teaching environment. Children express more through their bodies than they yet can through words. They deeply appreciate it when their bursting need for expression receives your attention.

Physical educators can benefit by supplementing lessons with the noncompetitiveness of creative movement. Allow children to vent their physical steam under your guidance: They will respect movement they create and gain appreciation from their peers. I make this promise to physical educators: As your pupils discover the ability to express themselves in movement of their own devising, they will develop self-confidence, self-reliance, self-respect, and, above all, the respect that comes from knowing that all people have unique ways of moving.

I have a hunch, borne out by some studies in psychoneuroimmunology, that there is an actual health benefit from observing, as well as doing, movement improvising; that our lives are enriched and given depth by experiencing vicariously the emotional expression-in-movement of classmates. The power of this work stems from group attention and interaction—from learning to look, see, and be genuinely interested in other people moving in front of us and together with us. It is this group expressiveness that I think has therapeutic value. The most lasting gift that all participants take from the experience is the realization that our lives revolve mostly around what is *not* said. The nonverbal expertise we sharpen in class carries over into the myriad nonverbal cues that we respond to daily.

I come from the generation that formed the cradle of modern dance in the U.S. Few of us knew the far-reaching import of what we were doing. Our principles then were to demystify and popularize dance. When I began teaching in an effort to reach nonprofessional adults, I was reinforced by the responses of women to the fact of my being a professional dancer. They gazed at me with expressions of such sadness, such longing, such quiet frustration, as they spoke variations of Oh, how I always used to dream of dancing, or How I would like to dance, but I'm too old. What I want to tell both women and men is that students of movement improvisation can be any age and have any level of training, including no formal training.

The content of improvisation is drawn from every aspect of daily living. The goal of *Movement Improvisation* is to evoke the body's memories, inspire emotional responses, and build respect for the improvising group. I use composition, theory, and other dance skills to help students create the extraordinary by celebrating what they think of as ordinary. The potent messages underlying improvised movement study are that all human beings are creative and resourceful, that our bodies may be awkward and yet capable of transmitting utter subtlety, that moving in front of and with a group can be invigorating (instead of intimidating), and that a lack of formal movement training does not prohibit producing sequences of genuine interest to ourselves and to others. I hope my enthusiasm will encourage you to use this material in any way you can, no matter your background or future in movement.

Acknowledgments

I enjoy reading Acknowledgments. Here we see authors revealed as human related to other humans and learn for the thousandth time the enormous complex of people, skills, and management behind the printed page. So I want to say *thanks* to all, and *thanks* to Human Kinetics for truly being an author-oriented publisher.

Thanks to Judy Patterson Wright, PhD, acquisition editor for dance. She was the first to read, recognize, recommend, and root for the manuscript, and she led me with patience, understanding, meticulous care, and foresight through the wilds of the contract and the practicalities that begin a book's fashioning. *Thanks* to Holly Gilly, developmental editor, who bore her third child along with the manuscripts she was nurturing. If Holly's offspring receive the quick comprehension, friendly easing of needs, and appreciation of the mutual creative process with which she helped birth this book, we and the future generation are all fortunate.

Thanks in memory of my family. I feel fortunate to honor these attractive and remarkably ethical individuals whose principles, vivacity, thought, humor, and forward-looking views on the human in society provide an invigorating heritage for life and teaching. *Thanks* to my mother, whose artistry showed itself in painting, ceramic sculpture, poetry, music, and in the classic grace with which she moved to her last days. With rare independence she resisted the ballet craze most mothers of her time succumbed to. I am in lifetime debt to her for taking me instead to the greatest teacher of interpretative dance for children. I overheard Miss Larson remark that I had "the divine spark." This spark has informed all my later creativity.

To my beloved stepmother, whose students have carried her innovative approach to science education all over the world. In characteristic defiance of ageism, she became a member of my dance classes along with far younger participants. It was she who observed what was developing as my special field and commented, "You have no right to keep this information to yourself." I immediately started to gather the ideas, sketches, and recollections of class incidents that this book is based on.

To my father, Phi Beta Kappa, logician, Renaissance man, who paid genuine and unwavering respect to my mind and person from childhood on, and who imbued me with his positive approach: If something has to be done in your field and you don't see it being done, you must do it yourself.

To my husband, gone so young, whose avant-garde taste and skills evoked my wonder, and whose legacy of love and its pervasiveness in my being makes me the kind of person—and teacher—I am.

Loving *thanks* to Professor John Stachel and to Arnold Edson, the two who always ask; to Professor Erna Lindner; to Barbara Melson, ADTR and Deborah Thomas, ADTR for their readings.

Thanks—for being interested, for being helpful, for just being—to Leon A. Arkus, Carole I. Binswanger, dear lusty esthete Ruth Bendor, Owen Davies, Vanya Franck, Professors Gaby Friedler and Dorothy Gregory, Bette and George Garfield, Harriette Moskowitz, Alicia Pauka, Mary Pelkey, Alice and Beatrice Rosenbaum, Tasie Russell, Dr. Laura Siegel, Bernard Zollo.

Thanks to Dennis M. Dreyfus for casting his critical eye on the earliest draft and pronouncing approval. To Dave Engler, who encouraged, "Pour it out." To Leonore C. Hauck for zooming in with friendly enthusiasm, adding polishing touches from the distillation of her long publishing career. To June Salm who, after decades of hearing about our work, only recently observed a studio class for the first time and wrote a deeply felt tribute to the poignancy, power, and revelation she hadn't anticipated.

Thanks to all my students, and to those who directly had to do with the book: Debra Bernhardt, for desiring to read the completed manuscript before its submission, and Ronnie Lichtman, for a later reading; Bruce Sherrill, whose clear appraisal and incisive advice flood light through decision-making and whose joyful and sensitive caring weaves bright threads into delicate durable fabric; Brenda Suler, who made us so proud as a national gold-medal competition winner, for her valued art time and expertise; and Carol Woolverton, who contributed technical assistance at her desktop firm in Lexington, MA.

Thanks to students' children whom we have watched grow up over the years they've joined in with us at Workshops: Alexander Bloom, Megan and Nicole Ferguson, Joshua Kurchin, Michael McHugh, Andrew Rizzo, Star and Vanessa Soudan, Gillian Williams, and Jonas Woolverton, and to the children yet to move around with us.

Now, as in every event of ours since August, 1990, let's form a movement circle to remember and celebrate Gregory Roegler, who for 10 years lent his dignity, grace, love, mischief, humor, imagination, and analytic depth to all our doings. Brilliant playwright, devoted student and classmate, you are ever with us.

And finally, a tribute to one whose longtime interest and belief in the value of our work has helped bring it into print. How can I—and everyone who will use this book—ever thank Professor Judith B. Alter.

Judy and I met on the East Coast—when her children, now grown, were very little—brought together by a mutual friend, Lisa Bennett, then director of a cultural center in California. Expressing her interest in the work going on in my studio, Judy urged me to let her organize my prolific, unsorted, and unclassified material. After some years she overcame my resistance to infringing on her busy schedule by convincing me that overseeing graduate students' theses is what she does all the time. "Trust Judy" became our by-phrase.

After the initial stage inspired by my stepmother's instigation, it is Judy who has seen this book through in every sense. All of you who have ever had Professor Alter as an advisor know what happens. Judy not only brought manuscript and publisher together but also has smoothed the way forward ever since. Each time I wanted to withdraw from the exigencies of rewriting, proofreading, and so on, Judy was there, either coaxing over long-distance phone from the West Coast or standing by actively in person. She is every writer's dream. From having written four books of her own, she knows each "step" along the way, from contracts through corrections. Prodded by Judy's enormous vigor and concentration, know-how and brilliance, we have pored over paperwork and enjoyed laughter that almost blew the paper away.

Though I've always expressed my appreciation to Judy, there's something I haven't told her that I would like to state now: She teaches improvisation and has a dance background similar to mine. But she *never* has indulged in any comparison; she has always only grasped the import of what emanated from me, respected it, and worked with that output until it crystallized in the integrity of my own words.

The teaching method described herein is built upon deep personal attention, to helping each individual express himself or herself. For you to know that this book was produced with the same respect for the individual as goes into teaching improvisation itself is a delightful introduction to the pages ahead. Bravo, Judy! And bravo, the quality–attention method of teaching!

A special note about the art work in this book: Rochelle Robkin teaches art in the Wisconsin school system. Though she also has a dance background, it should be encouraging to all of you, no matter your skills, that these drawings are one person's imaging and improvising throughout, based completely on her reading of the text. Rochelle has never been my student nor seen any of my classes. She has let her pen roam freely, producing sketches as she was so moved. We chose to use her illustrations instead of photos to maintain a suggestive, rather than a role-modeling, atmosphere.

*P*ART I

What Is In This Book?

I would like to open this book the way I open the door of my studio to you.

I hold the door wide in the well-lit hallway. I face you directly, and I smile as I extend my hand. A whole battery of reflexes and life experiences come into play the moment we meet. I am attempting—even before I greet you by name—to convey that you are welcome, that I will strive for your trust starting from this moment, that I am looking forward to our working together.

My intention is to be cordial, but my warmth will be tempered by an instant appraisal of your "intimacy tolerance"—the gauge that tells us whether a person is likely to be turned on or off by a whole range of the most delicately graded temperatures of person-to-person acceptance, of human exchange, of social communication.

You in turn would be reacting to me: taking in my demeanor and, even while listening to my words, using the most primitive element of judgment—observing nonverbal conduct—to estimate the movement and manner of this stranger and the safety of the environment.

This very interplay is what we are here to discuss and, as I invite you to sit with me facing the open studio floor (a space that invites movement to happen), we would each be making nonverbal adjustments to the other even as we pay attention to our subject.

And what a subject we have set ourselves!

Expressive movement, improvised movement, imaginative movement—movement that comes from the core of one's being. Movements for which there are no words in any language. Movements that, originally spontaneous, have become increasingly restrained and suppressed by society's strictures.

We are here to study this most intimate aspect of physical activity not only to free it but to develop it further, as more sophisticated communication, through that elusive and intangible medium—creativity.

How are we to approach this delicate area, the hunger for yet fear of physical freedom? How are we to make the body available to its occupier as an expressive partner for a lifetime?

Nonverbal communication relates us to human beings all over the world, in the present and in the past. Throughout history people have expressed life in some form of organized movement. Once upon a time, when the whole world danced, men, women, and children connected themselves ritually to the rising sun, the setting moon, the elements, the seasons, and every aspect of plant, animal, and human life.

Our throats produce sound naturally, and we train this sound for speech and song. Our bodies produce movement naturally; we can use this movement to enjoy and strengthen ourselves, to understand and encourage each other, to be alert to all that threatens us, to act quickly and freely with others toward mutual goals.

We do not have to be taught to improvise; this primitive form of expression is still used by us every day. It is an intimate human attribute, the nonverbal means by which we live. Our bodies react involuntarily—we express ourselves, reveal ourselves, unite and protect ourselves. What we do have to learn is how to read and clarify these nonverbal messages so we can know how we tick, who we are and what our needs are, and how to generate the energy and assertiveness to get these needs met.

For example, from the time we arise in the morning and throughout the day, our bodies are expressive. Even when we are by ourselves, going about our chores, we may find hand cupping chin, finger pointed into cheek as we muse, as we wonder how to solve or accomplish something. Alone at one end of a telephone conversation, we find ourselves gesturing. And talking face-to-face, our hands and body and face suddenly—in a way not planned, not even in our awareness—emphasize, illustrate, enhance our verbal utterances. Whether with familiar persons in our own homes or in public places with strangers, we form immediate impressions of how people feel or what they need or what they want us to do by the articulation of their silent body movements. We have to be utterly aware of these intentions of others so that we can react with appropriate sympathy, aggression, flight, or cooperation. And for the simplest example of an everyday emotional improv, note that it is unusual for a human not to express some physical reaction to horror, shock, surprise, pity, or shame.

What Is Improvisation?

to improvise:
1. To prepare or provide offhand or hastily; extemporize
2. To compose (verse, music, etc.) on the spur of the moment
3. To recite, sing, etc., extemporaneously
4. To compose, utter, or execute anything extemporaneously
[from the Latin *improvisus* unforeseen, unexpected]
—*American College Dictionary* (Random House, Inc.)

*What improvisation is to me is having an idea or a feeling and expressing it nonverbally. It's seeing where the idea takes me—seeing what grows out of it. As long as you can hold an idea in your head, whatever you do has beauty to it. It never looks phony. And you don't do things that are just done to be done. They're done because that's where the idea inside takes you to.**

Improvising is an experience common to all. It has the connotation of putting something together creatively, generally without much warning, in response to an immediate need (more water extends soup for unexpected company, curtains make a skirt for a Cinderella).

In movement it evokes that which is free, spontaneous, unpremeditated, informal, impulsive, unrehearsed, unplanned, not thought-out. It is a form of physical activity that does not require any previous training because it assumes that we all live by practicing the recognition and performance of nonverbal cues. Whether people think of their immediate physical responses as skills or not, a reconsideration would make them realize that many gestures and movements they have become accustomed to using are the wordless communications of life. And people get better and better at communicating as they find that others understand their nonverbal cues more smoothly and effectively.

In the study of movement improvisation, we observe immediate physical responses to a stimulus, a stimulus that could be a verbal suggestion, an impetus like music, or the behavior of another person or group.

Movement improvisation can be random (getting over or around a puddle while walking or running), reflexive (retracting from something hot or unpleasant), absent-minded (doodling), or intentional (a whole group moving over on a bench to make room for a newcomer).

---

*These italicized passages identifed by the dancing figures are unedited quotes from my students.

Movement improvisation includes reflexes, gestures, body language, mimicry, facial expressions, and signals. It uses all the learned motor behaviors: walking, running, leaping, skipping, hopping, jumping; all the body's natural movements: twisting, bending, reaching, turning; and all the body's emotional responses: shivering, shaking, drooping, shrugging, smiling, sagging.

We improvise movement to signal a discreet message; to convey an idea to someone who doesn't understand our words; to describe a form when we cannot reproduce it in writing; to emphasize a meaning; to dramatize our narrative; to leave a thought unfinished. We mimic animals; we exaggerate the measure of the fish that got away; we demolish a complex subject with a tiny wave of the hand; we ridicule what we are saying with outrageous or contradictory gestures. In every society there must be a gesture that means "words fail me."

Improvised movement can rise in response to a sound or rhythm; an emotion, story, or idea; or just from the desire to move, from the body's need to feel comfortable by yawning and stretching or to revel in its vigor.

In common understanding, most people think of movement improvisation as movement to music, done mostly by oneself or perhaps with a partner. You turn on a recording and just go—move around in a spontaneous, unrehearsed way to the music's rhythm and mood, or dance out a little story.

The movement improvisation described here is done without music. If you're composing a poem or story, or painting a picture, you don't think of doing it *to* music. Therefore, why is music necessary to compose one's own little dance or improvisation? In answer to a prospective pupil who asked why we don't use music (she loves to interpret music and finds it "sends

Greetings.

her beyond herself") I answered, "If you consider the body as an instrument, why not interpret the music of that instrument instead of having the music's composer set your rhythm, mood, and subject material?" I was taught to improvise to nothing but music and I found that this experience limited me. Now I choose not to use music.

There is nothing wrong with interpreting someone else's creation, or of using it as a setting for one's own. Indeed the larger part of our art heritage is based on interpretation; musicians and actors are largely interpretative artists. But in our present study we use movement that is initiated from sources that permit our own phrasing and timing. One of my students calls this "the music inside us."

By far the most important reason I do not interpret music is because a great many of the attributes of improvisation come from the relationship of the people in the group to the group as a whole. This relationship is derived from a diversity of tempos, rhythms, and moods. The content of our improvisations is not derived from interpretation but from creation, from the physical actualization of inner resources and life experiences—the imaginative and emotional material of our own lives and environment.

As a matter of fact, what my students and I have learned is that the use of music results in a different type of improvisation. Experimentally we have compared improvising in class to moving around at home to music by oneself. We found that the latter may be of deep inspirational character, may get rid of steam, work up a sweat, or be an accompaniment to romantic or sexual, imitated or learned phrasing. We found that moving spontaneously with others to music can be enormously satisfying and can rouse everyone to another level of human experience (as ritual does). We also found, however, that moving in accord with an outside source is not concerned with the emotional expressiveness that wells up when we follow our own "marching" and move to our own "drumbeats" and heartbeats.

Because the whole purpose of our work is to create fresh, genuine movement out of real life experience so as to compose dances, when we need sound we use nonverbal vocalization and the spoken word originating from our own subject matter (see #90, Poems in "Themes" section) and percussion instruments either self-played or as accompaniment phrased to our needs.

The concept with which we work is that by focusing on our present skills learned from life and by practicing them, we will develop a distinctive personal style and group cohesion. In a broad sense, one can consider the way one is taught by one's family to stand, walk, and carry oneself a type of life's dance training. We are further trained by imitating the mannerisms of elders, peers, and the media.

The human infant experiments with limbs and body—he crawls and makes attempts to stand upright. The young child continues to experiment until her movements are squelched. Our society gradually cramps and stifles movements until we lose our original freedom and instead become inhibited and self-conscious. In a society fearful of unconventional expressive move-ment, improvisation is a return to freedom; it is a revival of the natural ability of the body to produce a million movements of varying strength, intensity, nuance, and dynamic. In our work we will throw a wide net to catch the myriad of movements that swim to our eye from many sources: physiology, psychology, sociology. The movements we catch in this net—with the pur-poseful "hook" of an impetus—will be the nascence of dance, an art form that relates us to all of life. The impetus we use will come from sight, sound, and touch, and from verbal and nonverbal stimuli.

Improvisation is a revival of the natural ability of the body to produce a million movements of varying strength, intensity, nuance, and dynamic.

 *You bring to each topic your own background and your own thoughts and no two people are alike. They're unique in the way they perceive things. Also, their bodies are entirely different, and the movements will look different on [different] people.*

Each improvisation calls the body into an adventure of discovery. The unique movement in everyone can be characteristic or a surprising revelation and innovation. When you follow the lead of your body—its movements, qualities, and tempo—you get to know your deepest aspects. You relearn the nonverbal "remembrances" your body has stored up.

If a word is spoken and you let your body react to it immediately, it will unlock for you a whole series of movement reflexes, associations, and innovations. Suppose the spoken word is "sadness." Your eyelids may close, or your head bow, or your shoulders droop, or your hand cover your face. I just spoke that word to myself and felt my chest hollowing. Then I asked myself, "What am I feeling sad about?" My response was that I was experiencing a feeling of personal loss. I followed my body as this feeling flowed downward but then reestablished and lifted itself through chest and head. "I have come through sadnesses" is the message my body gave me. Then I let my body move from sadness to "life again" several times. Did you ever say something and then realize, "Oh, so *that's* what I'm thinking!"? It's the same with movements: We move and then learn what we have done and what our body meant.

Credo

Improvisation is not a product.

It does not have to have critical acclaim.

Or any kind of criticism.

Our pact is: Here, in this place, in this time, you can move as you will, as your emotions and spirits design, as your body wants to.

We're not going to be drawn into any comparisons.

Nor will I, as teacher, be drawn into being an authority on whether what is done meets with my approval or not.

We're all just going to accept what's done.

We open up our senses.

Your feedback will come not from us but from yourself, from what you did—from what you did not even know you were going to be doing.

Your security comes from the knowledge that "everything goes." Imagination and movement are encouraged to stretch ever further. When it is our turn to watch, we regard with interest what the body is doing; not whether what it is doing is likeable or not.

As these experiences accrue, freedom grows.

Central to the concept of improvisation is experiencing movement in the company of others. This coming together, [and] participating, feeds and stimulates each participant's creative processes. It's a social activity. It stands opposite "competitiveness" in the spectrum of human relating.

In improvisation, you can move as you will, as your emotions and spirits design, as your body wants to.

*P*ART II

Benefits of Movement Improvisation

Starting a newcomer on the most elementary improvs (such as "melting icicle," and "play with shadow") returns the adult to where she left off in childhood creativity and freedom. Then, as she gradually learns more advanced concepts and experiences the power of group positive reinforcement, she can go on to use this recaptured freedom to bring herself up-to-date in a mature, expressive life.

A student who was thinking of going into dance as a profession—possibly to perform—asked for my honest appraisal of her potential, especially since she was already over 25. I said, "You are attractive and interesting to watch as a personality, and of course you'd have to work on technique every day. But here in our improv classes in the studio we have become aware of the unique emotional coloring you give your movements. The exclusive emphasis on girlishness has been restricting your vocabulary. Only recently the *woman* has been coming through in your improvs. You're beginning to deal with the emotions that we usually associate with maturity (though children have all of these emotions, they express them differently). When you make this transition through your girlhood to maturity, although there may be many other good technical dancers, you will have exceptional quality as a performer. You will have this because, while you are adding to your improvs here to make them grow, they are growing *you*."

Every time we practice improvising, we improve the movement we need for our lives. The more we improvise, the more richly we live. When students are reminded that they learned to walk by first toddling, stumbling, falling, and rising again, they are more prepared to see that their spontaneous movements will develop in strength, endurance, concentration, and character with practice and repeated trials.

The atmosphere of the class—safe from criticism and moral or artistic judgment—and the concentrated and appreciative attention of group and teacher combine to create an invitation to be ourselves at our fullest. This invitation includes a tacit permission for the body and the mind to roam freely together. What a gorgeous release for the adult, who is always being tugged at to stick to one thing, nose to grindstone! From this adventurous voyage he comes back refreshed, confident, and ready to tackle life anew.

There is freedom to be oneself, no matter how zany, unconventional, or objectionable, as long as one stays within the confines of respect for the group. In improv it is actually impossible to imitate! One has to "do one's own thing." In moving around freely to an individual idea, one can use every cliche, every movement learned from somebody else or from the general fund of symbolic movements. But somewhere within that improv you make your own selection. Choosing what to do and what not to do is one of the aspects of artistry.

I want to be dancing about me and about people like me, wanting to be taught how to open up my body and do my own dance. For the first part of my life I danced literally and figuratively to everybody's tune: to my mother's tune, my brothers' tune, the church tune; I danced to everybody's tune. I think I went overboard in dancing to other people's dance. And what I'm finding is that nobody really knows but the person that's right there in that body.

Now it's my own dance, in a sense, but it's my own dance as an accumulating of all the dances I have known, or people that I have pulled from. It's nice to create a performance and have people pay and clap and applaud, but it's more about sharing the dance of life with people.

Every snowflake is different. No two persons in the world have the same breathing patterns. There are no two fingerprints exactly alike. Each person's creativity is unique. Each body is a unique instrument that can only play what you want it to. No one else in the world can create your improvisations; you are the instrument *and* the composer.

One of the artistic skills that is learnable in improv class is how to make transitions from one choice of movement to another. It is the way you make these transitions that leads to the development of personal style; how you go from one thing to another is one of the elements of style. Transition is what the stage director is constantly seeking when stage "business" is set; it is an inherent part of dance movement.

Learning to move with movements of one's own rather than given movements, and regarding these movements seriously and with attention, makes self-respect and esteem for others grow. Moving to a creative idea involves the whole person—body, mind, imagination, personal history, and social relatedness. Concentration allows you to experience your self most genuinely and completely. Body movements often express the essential self more deeply than the words we utter.

We jest among ourselves that there are moments in life when one wants to throw up one's hands and call it quits. But when we improvisers throw up our hands, this gesture is just the spur for some more creative movement! If you don't express your life, who will? Wherever there is suppression, other means are found to resist it. The body seeks to silently retain what the individual or group cannot express openly.

An historical illustration of this kind of nonverbal resistance is a folk dance incorporated into the Yugoslavian tradition. It is a silent circle dance, done by men and women to commemorate resistance to a tyrant who forbade verbal communication. The people met in the forest and, holding hands in the circle, expressed their unity with each other through noiselessly and wordlessly moving together. Given the courage, we can break another kind of suppression: unshackling ourselves from old movements and trying on new ones. "Freedom," "confidence," and "better feeling toward myself"— these are benefits mentioned over and over again as rewards for the regular practice of improvisation. In the interplay of mind and body, group and person, we rediscover movement as an ally for every aspect of life.

I like being "on my own side," reflecting in action what I really believe in rather than what is expected of me. Being genuine.

Over the past 8 years, improv has provided me with a "place" where I bring myself to an awareness of myself, the "me" that gets lost or neglected during the course of just living in the world.

Here we're committed to our own growth and change as individuals and as a group.

Movement improv makes us physically more interesting; revitalizes the body.

The end result of improvising that I've experienced is

greater confidence; [a] deeper understanding of myself and others; more effective, assertive behavior; a sense of freedom and empowerment.

I've come to class in all kinds of states, but always get my "second wind." The class gives me energy; things look better, are not so bad. You learn not to give up on yourself. The people and the "play" in class can introduce you to something else and is very good.

Regina wrote this in a poem: "What I do in class is a me known to solitude, unconfessed."

I "lost my head" in the best sense of the phrase: I learned to say to myself, "Let go of your mind," and to acquire the discipline that goes with doing that.

This is a place where I can just be, where I am accepted, where my sensitivities are not criticized.

I've learned to go into my artistic self, to trust my inner life and impulses, allowing myself to touch and be touched by others—both physically and artistically—with a growing awareness of what intimacy is.

I've discovered that my creativity is invincible; that it is my salvation, my joy, my sadness, my richness, my life.

I've been getting to know myself in a new way, and growing in confidence, self-reliance, and self-expression. It's clear to me that working with our class has been an integral part of that growth. It's enriched my life and sense of self.

Improv sheds light on my thinking and helps [me] clarify my feelings and go where my heart is.

Sometimes words are inadequate to express how deeply we feel about an experience. I know that I came to the right place at the right time.

Benefits from improv: a different perspective, an outlet for emotions, a means of finding new understanding and using the body to release tensions instead of holding them in.

I really feel I've developed confidence in terms of my body. Going to school or working, you develop confidence in different areas: in your intellectual ability and your ability to organize. But not necessarily being able to handle your body. There really isn't much expression with your body: You walk up and down the stairs, you cross the street, the most you do is drive a car.

I feel now that this kind of movement can't be separated in my life; it's become part of it. It's given me a way to express—and I have difficulty expressing verbally. The fact that I've stuck with it has given me confidence.

So you see, through creative movement we receive so much, and this is what I share with you in this part of the book: the benefits individuals and groups gain through improvisation, how improvisation enhances creativity, how it helps those who move integrate artistry into their lives, and how it can help free us from fears and inhibitions.

Benefits of Improvisation to the Individual

When one is doing, or even viewing, movements that arouse some feeling, the very recognition that one has such feelings is important. The practice of improvising makes one recognize one's own feelings and those of classmates, making those feelings significant and worthy of attention. Thus, improv makes one aware of one's feelings and strengthens them in the process.

Emotions, Confidence, and Self-Reliance

The benefit I hear most often from students is that they have grown in confidence. They have learned to move not only in front of but with others without being self-conscious or shy. It is surely an admirable benefit that improv reinforces personal empowerment and confidence in social interaction both in and outside of class. In improv students learn to trust their judgment in leaving old, worn-out, meaningless, or hollow habits of movement behind and taking on those that truly represent them. From attending to their own needs instead of having movements given to them, improvisers reawaken and extend imagination and creativity. This creativity carries over into other aspects of life. It makes individuals aware that they have a style as distinctive as a fingerprint because their movement vocabulary is developed from their own lives. While expressing meaningful subject matter, they get a taste of the whole world of movement they can find in their inner resources.

Improv class is particularly helpful in relieving the pressure on ambitious students—those who have to strive to support themselves, or who have to compete either socially, professionally, or artistically. These students are released from stress when they are involved in the improv process.

Some of my students have been in the dance world and know how competitive it is. When they are in creative movement class, however, they are expressing their own emotions in motions of their own, utterly free of the stress of comparisons.

A student once confessed (and she was confessing this for many others, as it is not unusual) that she was always a little unsettled when she first started coming to classes, wondering how she was going to do. Gradually, however, she lost all sense of anxiety and now comes with great ease of heart, looking forward to whatever movement experiences are in store for all of us together.

The worst moments were when I was so tense, and there was Susan in the class, with such a beautiful body and all, and I was just feeling like a piece of lead, and it was a real effort. But then I had like a breakthrough with anger—when I was angry enough to express it in appropriate ways and didn't have to sit on it.

For me, from my core, pain is much easier to express: pain and sorrow and grief. Anger—sometimes I'm into it and sometimes I'm not.

You have to keep things pent up and then finally you let it go, and it feels so good—even if they're things that are not so pleasant to talk about. Well, the same thing is true with your body movements; I feel that I've released something and that a certain amount of tension is gone. Calm is the best word to describe it. I've just finished something, and it was good, and it helped me and it was a release, and there it is.

In one improv tonight, Dana and Miako had a theme of showing anger at each other. Usually Dana is so reticent about expressing, but she got that look of anger. And I looked at her and I thought—oh, you know, her whole face—she looked different to me. Her face looked different. And she looked so pretty when she did it. Plus, she was moving. She looked angry and it added a dimension to her that she didn't have previously, to me. After two years, she suddenly came out of her shell.

When I have a serious commitment, the emotional reality of it is such that to let my emotions guide me through something spontaneously is something I'm freer to do.

If I feel very tired at the beginning of class and, say, the improv is about tears, you can do a wailing kind of thing that takes an enormous amount of energy or you can do a small cry, a small sadness. You make it what you want to make it; you make it relate to yourself.

These are my thoughts about my body and emotions:
Humiliation, shame—Shrinking of entire body (a sucking and pulling in of upper torso); wanting to sink into the ground (knees buckling); wanting to cover my face and head with my arms.
Excitement—Body energized (movements contained within the framework; not expressed outwardly).
Anxiety—As opposed to excitement, movement is contained but trapped in the diaphragm. So experienced as a capsizing inward at the stomach level.

An out-of-towner took a class with us. With surprise she said—about having the experience of what we do: "It tells you how you feel!"

Because we don't discuss the subject matter of the improvisation or the emotions that inspire her, the improviser is left with her own quiet contemplation. I believe this is one of the greatest benefits of improvising. This nonverbal permissiveness allows the individual to know that her privacy is literally her own and that she need not feel compelled to reveal it or to respond to anyone who challenges her. What she has done is hers—and that is enough for her.

This self-appreciation, when practiced over a long period of time, assures a solid core at the center of each individual improviser's being. He learns that he has something within himself that he can rely on without anyone else's approval. He learns that his movement offering doesn't have to be appraised, evaluated, or even liked by anyone observing. He learns that it is he and he alone who has produced this improv and it stands by itself as his own production. Not only can he remain silent about what he has exposed to us in movement, but we enforce his right to silence; by refraining from asking, challenging, or probing, we tell him that whatever he did is accepted by us.

Self-reliance is not a result of being shut out of a group and having to fend for oneself. On the contrary, the group is safe for the individual no matter what she does (barring harm to others, of course). She gets used to thinking over her own movement experience and having her own judgment be enough. I am convinced that self-reliance of this kind is carried over into life outside class.

Identifying With and Observing Others

I enjoy one of the early excitements in students' lives. They rush in one day and tell us how much they identify with the movement they see in dancers, athletes, or skaters. All human beings respond kinesthetically, but the improviser begins to realize that the movements he is doing in class give him the illusion that he is moving along with the performers he sees on stage or on television.

Instead of seeing a dancer perform and saying to oneself, "Oh, I wish I could do that!" the improviser is saying, "Yes, yes, I know how that feels; yes, I can see myself doing that; yes, I'm right up there too." It is a thrilling visceral tingle.

Connecting the movements on that television screen to the movements they do in class, students are able to understand how well that movement is done and what has gone into the making of that professional excellence. These professionals become role models—not for competitive frustration, but for continuing boldly to express more and more in class.

There is no doubt that our eyes become keener as we watch what goes on in front of us in class each week. This watching becomes a skill that develops more and more. It also carries over into our lives outside class; we observe our friends, family, passengers in a vehicle, and strangers on the street with more comprehension of how those bodies are moving and how the parts of those bodies are relating to each other. Observation also includes being sensitive to other people's emotional states. All students tell me they begin to observe everyone with more attention. This type of observation is invaluable in theater training and to those who are graphic and visual artists. As we observe the movement around us in daily life with keener perception,

Greater observational skills are a benefit of movement improvisation class.

we become adroit in handling ourselves in relation to other bodies. We may also be inspired by the movements of other cultures and so become more expansive in our views of the world's peoples.

I've seen people increase the range of their ability to improvise. Someone like Winnifred: I think she can do almost anything right now; I mean can express a range from very light to very heavy things. I remember her from years ago and I don't think the number of emotions she did then was the same as what she can do now. I mean she can do anything.

GS: *It's nice you can see that in someone else who's in class.*

In class I've experienced powerful improvs which have impacted on my life, both personally and professionally. I was able to improvise in an open, free way which has led to new insights and strength, due to a safe, permissive environment in which to work and discover.

Once getting over the fear/discomfort of being "watched"—and possibly being judged and criticized—I was able to accept and appreciate other classmates' undivided and respectful attention as I moved about emotional/social issues of my life.

It's quite helpful to be able to get up in front of everybody. It helps me and it helps other people. It's a good exercise for me because, just as I need to get into my own image, I do get into their own images.

What I get out of watching the others is that I enjoy sharing their experience. And feeling a oneness, a connection with everybody. That we each have different ways of expressing, that each of us has a personal style.

Vicarious Experience

Studies have been done about the effect of watching television on children, on groups, and on crowds. I would like to do a study of the effects—upon those of us who watch—as one after another, and then the whole group, move in front of our eyes in improvisation with genuine emotions. I believe we would discover that this has a health-giving kinesthetic and emotional effect on us as viewers. I know that I feel a deep emotional enrichment from observing my students. Something in the process of physically empathizing makes me feel a tone in my muscles, a flow of coordination of limbs, and a heightening of the variety and reach of life.

I am sure that what people get in watching each other express themselves emotionally is a specialized skill in itself. It opens us all to the widest human range. Sensitive and sophisticated psychological and physiological testing is needed to gauge the wondrous vicarious benefits we get from soaring with the prima ballerina, revving up with the tap dancer, and gliding with the ice skater. But we don't have to wait to know how it feels. And that's enough proof.

When we're playful, we're also engaging others in the playfulness.

A lot of what we feel is infused with humor. And humor isn't just jokes. There's a certain something about people being themselves that's humorous. I don't mean it's like laugh-out-loud humor, but it's—well, there's something humorous about people being themselves, between intent and results [laughs].

Trust

I would say that trust of the group as a whole is the basis for the greatest of all freedoms. What does it mean: to trust? It means to be laughed with, not against. It means we know we are not going to be hurt, that we are going to be safe. It means that if we have any vulnerabilities they will be protected. If we are weak personally we will draw strength from others, and we will lend it to them when it is their turn to need it.

What makes some people afraid of coming into a room where there is any kind of gathering? It's a fear of lack of acceptance, of being seen as unattractive, of negative response. After several months of weekly classes, I remember Nancy coming in one day and telling us that in her work as a photographer she had always been fearful of placing herself in certain positions relative to the crowd scenes she was filming. But after being with us, she had found herself going right up to the front and taking pictures of the crowd from the desired vantage point. She attributed her new comfort as a photographer to her safe feeling within our group.

The most highly skilled improvisers are those who have the most trust in their group. Secrets too deep for words or for sharing with parents, mate, best friend, or child are displayed in improv class because it is not possible to betray your intimate feelings to outsiders; these secrets can only be "told," or reproduced, in movement.

Laughter can be false, forced, grim, chilling, or cruel. The poems of Shelley remind us of the laughter that is "close to tears" and that "our sincerest laughter with most pain is fraught."

Members of improvisation groups lend strength to each other when it is needed.

We have to be careful, as we watch someone do movements that might be considered "funny" in the world at large, not to laugh. The improviser may be doing these movements as symbols of something that is hurtful to her personally. It is important to learn to watch sensitively and hold our laughter; when the improvisation unrolls, it may not be a laughing matter at all.

We also do not laugh when someone miscalculates a move or is thrown off balance and has to redo a step. This allows the improviser to make corrections in silence while maintaining his concentration.

From time to time, when it is impossible not to laugh, I remind the individual: "We're not laughing *at* you; we're laughing *with* you."

Once the 5-year-old son of a class member joined in with us and moved with such amazing accuracy and quality that we adults all laughed with delight. But that child ran away howling, his dignity offended at the thought that we were scoffing at his incompetence.

So, we have learned to hold our laughter until we know it is going to be seen as acceptance, as a sharing instead of as a criticism.

Of course everyone loves to laugh in response to delight, to being tickled pleasingly, to common appreciation of a phenomenon, and to a situation which gives us instant enlightenment. We have a lot of deep and genuine fun in improv class. One of our fun exercises, which can even be used as a party game, is the theme: "Bodies don't lie." In this improvisation we use actual spoken words, to show how we say one thing while our body is saying another. One person might shake another's hand and say, "Oh, I'm *so* glad to see you" while looking wildly around for escape; or, one person might offer, "Let me help you" without budging or making any attempt to help.

One memorable improv consisted of two women students rolling around on the floor while keeping up a conversation in forcedly normal tones, trying to top each other about how adorable their children were. Improv provides conditions, gives permission, and creates an atmosphere that encourages adult play in order to enhance life's petty and profound comedies.

I understand when a beginner in improv has uneasiness or hesitation because that's the way I felt when I began. The first time I came to class, I just sat back because my heart was, you know, beating. It was like being called on in school. And it was reassuring that the first things we did were group things, so I didn't feel I was the only person doing something. But as you continue to do it, you really feel more comfortable. It's a gradual process.

I'm a lot freer to do anything I want because I don't care what people think of me now, or how I look, as much as I used to.

I remember one solo. I was a little shy. You had brought out some of your scarves, some fabrics. And for some reason, the idea of dancing with fabric intrigued me. The fabrics were very beautiful, very glowing, very sensual. I remember running over and grabbing one—as opposed to being very shy and reticent about getting up and moving in front of the group. I don't remember the improv, but just about being excited in working with the fabric. I was able to allow my body to be more flowing. That was nice.

Though I danced before, it was intimidating to come to the first class here tonight. I was scared. I felt I couldn't do it. But one thing that was so incredible: The two things we worked on—the shape of our arms and moving our hips—had been really the two most difficult things for me; it never used to feel right. But tonight there was something different from the way I'd ever been introduced or exposed to it before. You had a way of giving us an image, not just presenting the movement—because that intimidates. The way we broke the movements down for ourselves, that way you know the way it feels.

When I first started this class, I think if I was afraid of anything it was of having to move around alone. I didn't think I was well-enough coordinated to be able to use two limbs simultaneously, or to be able to do what I was told. But what has been surprising to me is that not only do I not feel afraid, but I actually can make those limbs move together.

When I found that many in the class just did other jobs, I couldn't believe it; I thought they were all professional dancers. So when I left, I knew I could do it too, and that's why I came here to study. And I look forward to the improvs now, whereas it always frightened me years ago.

Relating to Others

When Chris imagines a ball in her hands and throws it to Demetrius, he knows it's a "ball" and can then choose to catch and play, rather than to turn away and disregard the imagery. But when the imagery is accepted not just by one partner but by an entire group, the cooperation of that group to hold the same image together is extremely powerful.

Of course, when that cooperation extends over into "real life" and at the end of a class I find all my props and fabrics and percussion and other gear has been quietly put back into the carryall in which I brought them, so that I don't have to do this by myself, I am touched beyond measure.

Unique in the class is that you can say no. It's not a big deal there. This is just the opposite of what I experience every day. So I can and do use the feeling of being able to say no outside of the class too, as a carryover. It's OK to say no. You can say no in the world and not be afraid.

Expressive movement is a door opener. It's not just what you do yourself, because we set things off in other people too. If you begin to move more freely, something comes through from the whole person and people are going to respond. The way you move is going to say something like, "Hey, you know, I'm not going to be used in a manipulative way."

What makes creative movement so interesting is its ability to tie itself into and/or perhaps change what goes on in our daily lives. You tend to release a lot of your pent-up problems through your physicalities, to lighten a lot of frustrations and anger.

I've been doing little movement improvs in the shower, and standing differently while brushing my teeth.

An actor: *I've been bringing the safety of our class into auditions.*

A dance therapist: *I find a real connection between my attitude towards my pregnancy and my becoming a mother with having been able to release these feelings in our work in class.*

A few weeks ago you said something about using an improv to perhaps loosen the way I hold my head. You planted a time bomb that keeps going off. The head is a heavy part of the body; it's also the thinking part, and holding it rigid not only affects movement a lot but says a lot about what's going on. I've found that just loosening the way I hold my head affects everything. And I'm making discoveries in walking: If everything is in balance, walking is very easy.

I'm in therapy and it helps being able to focus and deal with a theme that is coming out in therapy. It's a concrete and good way to work things out; a double help, bringing it back to my therapist, so it goes both ways.

The class sometimes brings the lighter side out and sometimes the darker. Opens up something else to happen. Gets me out of the stuck place. I take the feeling of this opening up, of possibilities, out of the class with me.

A social worker: *I am always interested in learning new ways to work creatively with patients. I've gained insight as to how to create a safe environment. It also reminds me what a vitalizing force creativity in my own life is and of the "healthfulness" of respect for one's own internal "music."*

On a day-to-day basis there are frustrations you really never can express directly and you may feel like tearing your hair out. When I bring my daily experiences into class, it gives them a new meaning for me and I take them out into my life.

A professional actor/director: *When one does some unforeseen movement in an improv, that movement might not only be a revelation, or lead to more insights in the improviser, but there is a "resonance" afterwards.*

A dance therapist: *A new outpatient came to a session and was very distressed because she hadn't brought what I call her "self-defining" guitar with her. She was terribly fearful and hostile until I made a suggestion inspired by one of our recent improv classes: I suggested that everyone improvise playing—nonexistent, of course—guitars.*

The floorboards of the house are creaking because I am improvising so many and varied leaps of joy. And in the kitchen, the sweet potatoes for tonight's party are being whipped to a froth they hadn't dared dream about.

I know that I come here to keep reinforcing my feeling of being OK, of being part of the human race.

I think you get a window into the other person's world.

I've become much more aware of other people. I especially like that exercise we do with two people passing each other by, again and again. I've always enjoyed looking people straight in the eye. That's part of the honesty that one projects on that little journey back and forth across the floor.

People just grow—like the night we first came and tonight. [She turns to a classmate and says,] "Now, Fay, you have so much more confidence in your lower back than you did initially. That gives me a lot of pleasure to see my classmate moving that way."

What happens sometimes is that I find people I didn't think of as beautiful turning very beautiful. And then I'm "unstereotyping."

I remember recently, when Pat and Al did an exercise, Pat could have gone off and shined, but instead he really helped and worked with Al to bring him out. It's a nice feeling to see other people in a very subtle way helping other people.

Our social set of movements for the purpose of communicating with others is utilized from the moment we awake (if our dwelling arrangements require interaction with family or housemates) and no matter where we roam. As public communication, both speech and nonverbal activity can be subject to misinterpretation. But the way we practice improvising in our class makes it possible to avoid most miscommunications. In class there is an interested group watching and attention is focused on accepting whatever is being presented by the communicating improviser—quite a different atmosphere from that of the world at large.

Yet another dimension of communication takes place within ourselves. Like the words we sometimes speak that give us an insight into what we are thinking, first we move, and then we discover the feelings that inspired our movements.

Fantasy and Freedom

Fantasy is a uniquely human ability, a combination of imagery, imagination, and storytelling. We usually think of fantasy as the opposite of reality. But when you put on a mask to go to a party, you are a real partygoer and your costume is accepted by others, even though the use of that mask is an act of fantasy. Fantasy may use images of real things.

A daydream takes elements of real life and fashions them to the daydreamer's taste. With this kind of fantasy, one can dream of what one would like to have and make the circumstances ideal.

Then there is storytelling, in which children tell each other and anyone who will listen stories real, imagined, or a combination of both. There is an aspect of skill in some storytelling. I remember my closest girlfriend, when we were 8 years old, often engaged in telling stories she would make up. We all listened to her spin these tales, and she grew in skill as she received our rapt attention.

Fantasy can take us to real places we've never been to and to places that don't exist. It is harmless until it is believed and passed off as fact. Even then, the harm it does can be of varying degrees. You are on a trip and telling a fellow traveler all about yourself—a self you are manufacturing right then and there, for the purposes of being interesting or romantic, or of exhibiting some other desired trait. This is merely a masquerade for the storyteller until it seems like reality and continues to be passed off as such. Some who tell different "facts" about themselves to each person they talk with are unsure who they are themselves, or so hate who they are that they must present a more acceptable persona.

Because improvisation in movement is a combination of a moving body and an imaginative mind, both working together, the teacher gives the improviser unbridled license. Fantasy, after all, approximates the art experience; this is what we in the audience bring with us when we go to the theater. Fantasy also permits those with no formal background in any of the performing arts to "pretend," to become something other than self. This process draws fresh and genuine movements from the body, which the imagination of all of us who are watching follows.

The improviser may use her imagination to become an ice skater and ends her improv with a triumphant pose, as if it is the climax to a fantasy display of virtuosity at the Olympics. We, as audience, support this fantasy to the hilt. Or, the improviser may be a ballerina making extravagant bows to her captivated admirers; we in the studio with her are even moved to throw her bouquets. All fantasy, all enjoyable.

Fantasy expressed in movement gives the mover the illusion of having been through the experience. And why not? If one can't have the actual experience in "real" life, why not approximate it so that the body feels as if it has been through that experience? This is one of the good things to come out of an improv class. The improviser can take bows for a highly skilled performance without the benefit of practicing day in and day out for a lifetime (one doesn't have enough lifetimes for that!).

Benefits to the Group

In each class each student builds her own non-oral tradition by using material from her own life, building her own tradition within her body. Even in a few class hours a week the student can experience, and the group can view, what amounts cumulatively to the physical, social, and emotional history of that particular improviser.

And in a yet more remarkable development, the group acquires its tradition of movement seen and fashioned together. The group's culture is fed by the recollection of individual and group contributions. Members influence each other's freedom and styles. In the course of regular group contact, our familiar movements grow in beauty and power; the body's expressiveness becomes eloquent, we develop appreciation for our differences, and a strong group emerges.

The group accomplishes what individuals can't: mutual awareness and sensitivity. Group awareness is experienced in the bodies of improv class members. There is delight in picking up cues that mold personal interpretations into one group composition. Genuine mutual appreciation arises for what is created together.

This is a rare type of group in that its members are alternatively audience and participant. The group encourages those who are timid to blossom because we give respect to that individual's potential as we all begin to glimpse it. The group in turn is strengthened by each one's increasingly invigorated confidence.

Group-related people share a genuine intimacy, for what is intimacy but knowing and caring? We go beneath appearances, beneath the superficial to learn what is underneath. That learning gives us sympathy—and, sometimes, awe.

The appreciation for each member's unique quality is sharpened. And, as individuals become less constrained, the group becomes more cohesive, more coordinated. Group power extends our individual confidence and creativity. Self-consciousness is replaced by warm communication with the audience of fellow students *because* we take turns being improviser and audience.

The theory of all our work is that the group is the powerful factor in our expressiveness, because it tests our communication abilities; it gives social sanction, approval, and appreciation. Fellowship and cooperation are joined with the aesthetic in relating each to the other within the group. If a wheel has to be turned, it is turned by all hands, and no question is raised about the hands except that they lend themselves to turn.

The Power of Group Imagination

When a group of people simultaneously work on imagining, the power of the individual is amplified in the atmosphere this activity engenders. In the warm-up period of each improvisation class, students learn to regard their bodies as instruments through which expression is produced. It takes many instruments to make an orchestra. In collaboration creativity, members of a group pick up sparks from each other; the sparks are fanned as the group creates, and the flame emerges as all catch fire.

When a group thus creates movement together, this has been a creative event. It has occurred. This was *it*. Each individual has been made to feel larger than life; one of us is transformed into all of us. Group power brings a surge of pride in unity.

Respect

In a nonverbal activity people have a different relationship. Caring and respect shows in the eyes, even toward people who outside the group we might be annoyed with or alienated from. Here the respect is for what we produce and how we relate.

We respect differences in interpretations. We respect each other's growing freedom. By itself, a body can be trained to be remarkable in technique and in quality. But that body in a group is tuned in concert with and in response to the others within the group.

Trust

Trust is the single key to a group's confidence. You can't climb a mountain unless you test each step for firmness and solidity. The trust in a group must permeate each individual member so that she or he can express *anything*. And then there is that uncannily amorphous area in which the members trust themselves to interact when it comes to a group venture. It is actually impossible to embark on any group improvisation unless each member of the group is confident that the others are as interested, as committed, as concentrated as she or he is. The heat of concentration can be maintained only if all are equally permeated with the same theme, if all are lending themselves to it wholeheartedly.

Trust permits individuals to lose any fear of relating to the group physically, of being touched and of touching. People who think they are alone in their problems, who don't even reach out to others and with others, get permission in a sanctioned group activity such as improvisation to reach out, to ask for and give help. They are enabled to touch other hands and bodies in a noncommitted, nonsexual, nonthreatening way.

Trust enables group members to touch in a noncommitted, nonsexual, non-threatening way.

Recently one of my students said, "You're letting us touch much more than before." Startled, I examined my recent conduct. Actually it was not I who had "let" the group touch more often than before. It was that they, who used to continue the no-touch admonition I started them with, had become so friendly and trusting that they themselves touched more easily—with no words said or appraisals made by either them or me.

Variety

A group becomes more interesting and expands its horizons when it has diversity, just as a nation does that contains many ethnic cultures. When a group weaves all their cultural strands together it makes for a remarkably ingenious, colorful texture. Individuals of dissimilar technical and conceptual abilities all contribute toward the completion of one group composition. Their individual identities are reasserted rather than smothered within the group. There is excitement in discovering the wide variety of individual interpretations of a given suggestion or theme. Recognition of these individual differences broadens the group's basic maturity.

Magic

In every improvisation class we create magic. We do things ourselves that we never thought we could do. We do things as a group that we all marvel at. It's so beautiful and harmonious; we're all moving together as if we planned it that way. In each brief time together we create our ideal environment: a safe, strong group in which we move trustingly to enrich our expressiveness in relation to each other. It is amazing how quickly nonverbal activity can unify strangers into a group. I've observed workshops where people who have never met are rapidly welded into a cohesive mass ready to tap into its new connections.

I think the reason we become a group so quickly is that everyone is relieved on a profoundly deep level to be permitted and invited to become free. The taste of freedom is heady. It's an amazing delight to move around freely with people instead of distrusting them and keeping them at a distance. The shackles of nonfreedom fall away. People even look at each other differently in improv class!

The Factors of Group Power

In improvisation, we are not only given permission but are encouraged to move our own way, a freedom the outside world may deny us. No one person in a group could even attempt to improvise unless the whole group had created the environment for that improv to take place. It is because we all have created the ideal environment together that we think of ourselves as being movers and shapers. This is enough to give each one of us, alone and with the group, a feeling of power.

Caring, responsive, trusting, congenial, interested, united in purpose, sensing accomplishment, working hard together, knowing who we are—these are the attributes of those who develop and are developed by the group.

Enhancing Creativity

It's a process of some kind of mind and body communication, concentrating on a specific image and letting the body more or less lead the way without conscious decision-making or choice-making. It's a process of self-discovery, even as you're doing it. It's a spontaneous form of communication, coming from levels within the mind or the bone marrow.

I have a broad view of creativity, just as I have of art and artistry. I believe that all humans are creative and that we demonstrate that creativity in every aspect of our lives. In its most simplistic sense, art is creativity that is made up of choices.

Choices

The artist chooses color, shape, intensity, placement, contrast, juxtaposition, etc. In our everyday lives we all make choices. Choices of clothing for oneself and children are creative acts. The planning of a menu and making of a meal also necessitate choices, of what to prepare, what to buy, and how to put them before the eater. Cloth, eating implements, and the setting of the table are all choices.

Even the way we order the activities in our day can be considered creative. We choose to do one thing instead of another or to do one thing first and another thing second, third, and last. Using time is not only a matter of efficiency; it's a matter of weighing relative merits of different activities and discriminating between them.

The "Practical" and the Creative

I've interviewed many students about their creativity. Did they consider themselves creative as children? Do they consider themselves creative now? Most answered yes to the first and no to the second. What happened to that lost creativity? When asked why they thought they were not creative now, the same phrases were used by almost all: They said it was snuffed, stifled, "beaten out" of them. What a violent phrase, "beaten out"! Indeed, it feels like a violation to have our childhood creativity taken from us. Why does this happen to children?

In a large society it is more convenient to see the human being as static, docile, and conformist so that huge numbers of people can be kept in order. Creativity, because it implies change, is seen as a threat to that orderliness. Although we are referred to as individuals in society, our individuality has been stifled. Most people do not think of themselves as expressive, imaginative, or creative.

But what a powerhouse of creativity everyone has!

Thinking up new ways of doing things makes life, liberty, and the pursuit of happiness exciting. Creativity is an important ingredient of democracy. With it we can envision better ways of living together and share the knowledge of the world's people. Creativity is an enormously active venture of the mind, which constantly works to invent the new, the better, the different, and the beneficial.

A creative person doesn't just take something as given; he can change it, adapt it to other uses, distort it for effect, add to it or subtract from it, or wring humor or other emotions from it. How sad that we think our creativity has been crushed so that we deny and fear the very word. Movement improvisation begins where early restrictions were imposed and frees both mind and body.

As a child I was a very free spirit, wild and physically active. I loved to run and jump and try to fly. At age 5 I think I was most essentially the person I feel myself to be. So I've been doing what I can to move back to that very clear sense of personhood I used to have.

When I think of my creative abilities now, I stand a little taller [laughs]. There are times of the day when I think about class and I always feel good about it and look forward to the next one, to—you know—find out more about myself. I do things in the improv class that would never be called for in another class, even in a dance class. New movements come out in improvising.

Can Creativity Be Taught?

The question as stated implies that creativity is something inherent in the learner and that teachers can only impart further skill to those who already possess it. The very assumption of free compulsory education is that everyone can and will learn. On the basis of this premise, we attempt to teach our young minds an enormous range of "subjects." The area of controversy is not can we teach Johnny to read, but how to best accomplish this. The implication is not—as it is with creativity—that we can teach only those who already have "it" and disregard those who don't. If by "teaching" we mean taking the child's ability to learn to walk for granted and developing this potential into the skill of upright locomotion, let us also teach creativity and answer the question "Can creativity be developed?" with a resounding Yes! Creativity, like any other human attribute, exists in everyone; it needs only to be recognized, released, and reinforced.

Even when I feel something I've moved about hasn't quite been realized, at least something came out of me. It's a wonderful, wonderful feeling to know that something can always come out of you. It makes me feel that I have great depth—[long and hearty laughter] unrealized depth. And that is marvelous. And as for creativity: It can be developed, it can be learned, it can blossom. There's always a seed, and you can always grow a little bit.

The Creative Mode

In movement improvisation we tap into our gut feelings. What might be called mysterious or other-dimensional can also be seen as the human ability to shift to the creative mode in which our explorations, imaginings, and make-believe takes place. We may not know how to locate it in the brain, but we know it is there. We start something creative in motion and then that very motion "moves" us, sometimes leading us onto unforeseen paths. After much experience, rather than merely being mystified by this element we accept it as part of the process of improvising. We incorporate it as a welcome ally, an expected component, and a sought-after ingredient in the creative process. The shift into the creative mode is possible for everybody; we just need to learn how to access it.

One of the fascinations is the way each class member lets an emotion, a thought, an event from life simply drop into her body and move, without planning. It comes naturally and sometimes unexpectedly.

Then I think at times something else sort of takes over. There's a point at which I feel myself moving in a fashion that quickly, very quickly, outsteps my ability to imagine it ahead of time. It suddenly becomes something that I am rolling with or moving with, and there's a kind of ecstasy involved.

The experiences are in the muscles, and the memories are there, and if you begin to move, one perhaps suggests another. When you see people who have a very limited movement repertoire, rigid and patterned, they don't know what a gold mine their body is. So I kind of come here to dig up a couple of nuggets—not how high I can kick or how good is my turnout. It just means I've got something in me that can be said in no other way than through movement.

Dear Teacher

I pray you, please do not exclude anybody from the experience of this creative mode. If you truly see all your students as possessing it, it is you who will further unlock this mode for them. Your conviction that everyone has this ability will give them courage.

As for degrees of creativity, life is a matter of degree. We must help those who seem to have the least achieve the most they can. In movement improv there are no geniuses, and by the same token, no failures. One person's grief can be expressed in few movements; another can go on for many minutes with many more movements. Each has expressed the grief that possesses her and we honor both.

The Three R's of Freeing Students' Creativity: Recognition, Release, and Reinforcement

This book is about how to teach creative movement to everyone. The greatest thing you as teacher can learn is that this can be done. Those who leave your class still thinking they "can't be creative" may have reasons for thinking this, but their *ability* to be creative is not one of them. All people can be taught how to access this mode.

Recognition

The teacher's first task on the road to awakening creativity is to extol the variety of choices students make. This can be done by eliciting from them a simple familiar movement. For instance: "Say hello—without using words. Just *do* hello." These will probably be hand signals that function in our society as greetings (in other societies, people point to themselves as an

As a teacher of movement improvisation, you can help students unlock their creative mode.

indication that the departing one should come back). You will be able to spot variations throughout the whole class. I keep clippings of photos of public events in which all are reacting to the same stimulus; two persons are rarely doing the same thing. Recognize these variations and have everyone see how distinctive their own version of "hello" is.

Immediately point out: "Look how each and every one of you has a different way of 'saying' hello. That means it is your style." The students can see this distinctiveness before their own eyes, and will remark on the truth of what you are telling them.

With these tiny differences in movement, you can start the process of recognition by you of their differences and recognition by them of their individualities. This knowledge emboldens the students, who gain self-appreciation and look at what they have produced as something distinctive. They then can go on to make even more daring efforts as you call forth their responses to a number of stimuli.

Release

The teaching of movement improvisation does not hinge on showing or telling students what to do; rather, it involves giving them every physical and psychological means to liberate themselves from what they've been inhibiting, storing, and shoring up. Everybody has hidden movements. Positive encouragement from the teacher must accompany every new movement that comes from each student. The emerged movement is then ready for reinforcement.

Reinforcement

Having recognized that their choices of movements are part of their creative capacity, the process of your students' thinking of themselves as creative will have begun. This will permit and encourage hidden movement, emotions, and experiences to be released. These tentative motions—like any other newborns—need to be nurtured. Recognition that one *can* make a movement starts a ripple effect that then goes on to produce that movement; next we encourage that movement to grow.

These students' quotes illustrate many kinds of reinforcement:

I am working in a hospice and therefore my "Personal Stuff" was about death and dying. As I moved, I felt how I sometimes see what happens during the dying process, and that death is like looking at the sun: You can look at it for only so long before you have to turn away from it.

The essence of my movement was to feel intense pain, to move away from it and then feel extreme release

Movement improvisation gives dancers physical and psychological means to liberate themselves from what they've been inhibiting.

and comfort—two opposing sensations and emotions. After, Georgette had Pedro come to the center of the studio with me and [she] asked me what I wanted from him. I asked him to give me unconditional support and love.

In response to this, he did two different things. And it's amazing how opposite my behavior was toward him on the two occasions. His first approach was to walk over to me while I was doubled over in pain, and place his arm around me. I lashed out at him. His next approach was simply to stand beside me, assuming my same doubled-over position without touching me. I approached him. I placed my hand on his back. End of exercise.

After each one's "Personal Stuff," Georgette gives that person a "Reinforcement." Some examples from our last class:

1. We were asked to "admire" Bryan's movements— without touching him.

2. We had to keep Juanita from descending physically to the ground.

3. Terrence had to repeat his movement first with sounds, then without sounds. These were sounds he had been producing very audibly from his chest. We had been discussing the relation of self-produced

> *sound to our improvs, so he was having his own*
> *experience contrasting* making *sounds to accom-*
> *pany himself versus* not *making sounds.*
> 4. *As a group, we were to keep Ricardo from hitting*
> *the wall (as he had done in his improv) and then*
> *he was asked to keep each of us from hitting the*
> *wall as he had done.*

GS: *At the end of your improv, you were crouched on*
your knees, head down, hands beside your head, palms
turned upward. I asked the rest of the class to come and
take this "holding" position with you, and then for you
to come out and watch while they continued the kind of
movement you had been doing.
What was the effect of that?
  Annette: *It made me feel good, and feel good about*
what I was doing. I enjoyed watching them do it because
two of the people went a completely different way from
what I was feeling but one person stayed with my feeling.
I watched that person a little more than the others; I felt
my feeling was continued in that person's movements.

I just started class recently, and I look forward to it. You
get an opportunity to concentrate on aspects of yourself
that you don't ordinarily. Even just basically using mus-
cles you don't ordinarily use. So it gives you an opportu-
nity to be different from what you are all the time, every
day. Becoming aware of your body in a different way,
you feel a sort of self-righteousness: "I'm doing something
about it, aren't I?"

Concentration

At each class session, as students learn to hold a concept (a word or idea) in their minds to see what movements come out of the body, everyone becomes aware that the ability to express detail and nuance is growing.

Creative activity requires concentration, as the muscles are actually dredging up memories. The process of creating requires synthesizing relevant memories with the artist's inner vision and purpose. Creative concentration cannot stand to be interrupted.

We learned what an intense concentration we had been developing when Sally, one of our most skilled improvisers, returned to class after a long absence. She discovered that with lack of regular practice her ability to concentrate had been weakened. Her thoughtful comment was: "When I came down this hall that I have come down so many hundreds of times to our studio, I wondered if I could still do it [improvise]. Then, after the first improv, I realized that my concentration, which used to be so thorough, had become somewhat dissipated, and there were moments when I had to pull my mind back to the theme I was moving on."

When my concentration is on the idea—it's like, I don't play tennis but the few times I have, you know when you hit the ball smack right. I mean you feel it, and it's the same thing in moving: You know when you're moving and [are] not aware of your movements.

I learned—from watching Sharon—to deepen my concentration, both during class and during improvising. So that each thing takes all of my effort, not a half-effort. Twice the effort makes it twice as good.

Integration of Improvisation and Artistry

We live while constantly checking both inside and outside ourselves to find out, to define, and to appreciate what we are doing, being, and becoming. As infants we look to the faces that look at us; as children we look to others to see how well we are learning to walk, talk, and eat. As we grow, we use mirrors, psychology, and the eyes and ears of friends; we create the news and then run to the newsstand to see how the journalists have portrayed us; we go to the theater to see if we are on the stage; and we watch television to see how like or unlike others we are.

Music, colors, shapes, forms, and movement all flow into and out of us in constant interaction. We continue to use all of these things to determine who and what we are. This interplay between ourselves and the arts that we hungrily seek out, in order to clarify us to ourselves, is enough to keep us busy for a lifetime.

These have been my first classes in movement, and now sometimes when I'm home I create dances, playing with different ideas and imagining how I'd like to see them performed.

I've found that as creativity in one area opens and grows, it overflows into other areas. Creative efforts reinforce and develop each other. From improv I've used that creativity in art, sculpture, writing, and in my life.

Art's Aims

It is not the primary aim of any form of art to give emotional release. But one of the great releasing factors of art is that there are no boundaries. In art we can extend, magnify, distort, juxtapose, satirize, uglify, beautify, and glamorize; while being sacrilegious, unsanctimonious, saccharine, nostalgic, outrageous, and innocent.

We can keep in mind the various "rules" that each school of art throughout history has constructed. We have not only our present but all that has preceded us. We can abide by any one of these concepts of art, or become iconoclasts who challenge all and create the new.

Who Can Be an Artist

Everyone can be an artist, including a child or beginner, with one proviso: There has to be a "consciousness" involved with his or her activity. The child who dances around freely is charming, fetching, delightful. But she is artless if there is no concept involved in the child's mind as she performs an activity.

But both the beginner and the untutored—either child or adult—can have an awareness of something that comprises more than just the tools of the trade; that there is, in fact, a *striving* involved. The beginner with the paintbrush might decide to paint the flower in the vase; it's not just a mindless doodling. The untutored picks up a pen or goes to a typewriter and begins a short story, novel, or essay. But he immediately faces the question of selectivity—for all of art involves choices: What word, adjective, or adverb should I use? How long a phrase, sentence, or sequence? What about overall form, intent, and conclusion?

In the course of our day, we and those we meet tell each other about what's been happening to us, relating stories, describing people and places, relaying information, repeating dialogue, and venting emotions. This is all the material of art. But what makes it into art?

Improvisation Is the Springboard, Not the Art

I think of movement improvisation as a springboard into the art of dance, but unlike dance, improvs are not intended for an audience. Choreographers often use movements that arise spontaneously or are purposely experimented with as a reference for composing, adapting, and setting a performed piece.

Most arts use their own forms of improvisational and experimental bits and pieces as the basis of a perfected offering for an audience. Such examples from other arts follow.

Events and information can be woven into a documentary. Or, a written short story can become a scenario for a film. A professional storyteller can practice telling a story so often that he or she can tell it under any circumstances. Garrison Keillor says that he has so much background from being raised in a family of storytellers that he can start himself on a story and rely on arriving somewhere—he sometimes doesn't know himself just where until he comes to the end. And, of course, dialogue is part of all the plays ever performed. The playwright will intend words and actions for an audience and the actors will interpret and prune and change them for a performance.

I don't know why I was so surprised at how excited I was seeing myself on videotape for the first time. But now that I've seen the tapes I believe they can have a very important use. Many people are intimidated by dance or any movement as an art form. I have a lot of friends who don't go to these performances because they feel they won't understand. It's very uncomfortable to feel that way (I've experienced it) and can lead one to feel inadequate. "Am I missing something?" you wonder.

The wonderful thing about the tape is that we can see the process. Here an idea is being thrown out for someone to "catch." Here's someone's instant reaction to that idea, in movement. This brings the whole idea of nonverbal communication to a much more "graspable" level. And the fact that we're not all professional dancers makes it even more [easy to identify] with. I think it could really help people see movement as less remote from their own experiences.

The Art Conspiracy

If a group envisions itself as a flock of birds, all the members of that group see themselves and each other as birds, and the audience enters into their creative conspiracy. All use their powers of make-believe and fantasy in the tacit understanding that art is an activity shared by doer and viewer. "We believe!" cry those on the other side of the footlights when *Peter Pan* plays.

I was at a party the other night and somebody asked me, "What do you do?" But it hit me wrong and I just stuttered and didn't know what to say. The next day, when I was feeling good, I thought I should just have told her I was a dancer. I felt dancing was my other life, sort of my fantasy life, my fun life; it was something I didn't want to talk about.

Improvisation as an Art Form

Improvisation is not an art in itself; it is a seedbed for experimentation, trial and error, winnowing and retaining, chancing, and sounding. Every artist has developed a different means of using improvisation for summoning up the instantaneous and spontaneous and inspecting it for use and intent. What bubbles up is a means toward shaping art. The highly experienced artist may take what teems out of the brain or body and work with it toward an end.

The second form of improvisation is one in which the artist starts with a well-planned, rehearsed work and leaves a space within that work to improvise. An example is the jazz performer who stays with the rehearsed familiar tune and then trusts herself to go wherever led or inspired by that original tune. Or, the violin concerto where the eminent soloist departs from the composer's written score and provides a cadenza. This is space for the soloist to soar, unaccompanied by the orchestra, into variations of his own making and style. Break dancers never stop rehearsing, so that when they face a street audience they can each take off in their own distinctive ways.

Movement Improvisation and Art

The intent of improvisation in movement is not to crystallize or rehearse, but to free. The improvisation is the intent, as it shapes itself. I tell my students: "Skip around your own way" means to view once—and for no other, future purpose—what that human being will do, how that human being will skip, and how that human being will skip around. And that's all there is to it. The skipping *is* the improvisation.

Watch what incredible variations there will be in response to that one summons to "skip around." One can skip in place, straight ahead, in circles about the room, with the knees raised in front of the body, with the knees going out to the sides or back, quickly or slowly, daintily or rowdily, forward or backward, and so forth. ("So forth" is part of the improvisation too, if it takes one into activities other than skipping.)

Voilà, the improvisation is done! That was it. Each improvisation is a one time experience. This skipping was not done in the street, on a dirt road, on flat rock in the country, at home alone in a living room, or at a party. This skipping was done in my classroom, in the presence of classmates, under my intent. I shape and guide and inform with my intent to use improv as a basis for creating dances.

To help students grasp that improv is a seedbed of an art form, I objectify the improviser's movement. When the novice first stands on the floor of my studio I say, "Think of your body as an instrument through which you are going to express yourself.

"Now inspect this instrument. Look at every single little part of it, to see what kind of instrument it is and how it functions. Put your attention inside your body, your instrument, and see how the muscles and bones work. Go with this instrument and put every part of it to work in moving, so you can see the movement it produces, see its capabilities, see its potential."

Warming up the body is like warming up any instrument in the orchestra. Then the instrument is put into play, and the dancer can see how it interacts with other instruments. This broadens one's view of the body as an object and instrument.

From then on, as I observe each improv, I watch to see how I can introduce some art principle from the art of dance. I comment on form, line, tempo, direction, level, and dynamics. For example, perhaps an improv was highly charged with emotion and feeling. But I do not comment on this; instead I use the fresh, genuine movements that have come from that feelingful person and suggest (first pardoning myself), "I hope I won't offend the emotion you just expressed, but I want to bring in something objective—that the hand doesn't have to cover the mouth; it can be kept a few inches in front of the mouth, for 'stylization.' Or, I may give a class specifically about parallels, the use of studio and interperson space, or the use of "silence" (no movement in between movement). Or we may spend intensive time on opposition, transitions, turns, and the basic steps of dance—walking, running, sliding, gliding, hopping, skipping, jumping, etc. As the vocabulary grows, the understanding of both improviser and "audience" (fellow students) grows and eyes are sharpened.

When I thank the improviser, I thank her because we are using that human being's emotional material as another objective step in learning about movement as a source of an art form.

From this exposition, one can see how intent shapes the use of movement material. Intent in drama shapes communication with an audience; intent in recreation can shape movement into fun, team spirit, coordination, and a game free of competition. And in therapy, intent shapes movement to provoke emotion. Therapy aims to help people relate to others both physically and emotionally, and open personal secrets so that both therapist and client can probe them together.

We glide. We lift our sails and glorify the breath of heaven by letting it move us. When there is no breeze, we can create our own, because our bodies are meant to sail— and even in the droop of doldrums our imaginations have wings of their own. Perhaps we are at our best when there is no wind at all!

Rare birds of a feather, we scratch and soar. This is quintessentially human.

Freedom From Fears and Inhibitions

Most adults come to their first creative movement class anxious, some to the point of being terrified. Fears, like any other disasters, flood away reason and make us incapable of functioning normally. Students may bring inhibitions like these:

- Negative personal reactions to and experiences with teachers and other authorities
- Interactions with other adults in the "outside" world and even more revealing and intimate interactions with adults in the creative movement class
- Expectations of self in relation to an art form
- Physical inabilities to "keep up" and to follow directions
- Exposure of ineptitude
- Emotional deficits
- Social alienation
- Self-consciousness about the defects and proportions of one's body
- All the don'ts and repressions taught as good manners, decorum, exemplary conduct, and "getting along"

The fear of creativity itself, joined with the fear of clumsiness, exposing one's feelings, and basic doubt all make movement improvisation very threatening indeed.

I used to be frightened of improvisation. It's the fear: How do I know what to do with my body? You don't know how you're going to look. Is your thigh going to look very big or is your foot going to be hanging there with nothing to do? Do you have anything to say? Just the act of creativity itself. So it's not just the physical fear but the emotional fear. With a person who's never done improv before, I think the fear is not having anything to do; thinking one couldn't go into any depth.

Physique

It is not only women who are concerned about their bodies appearing clumsy, awkward, ungraceful, or "too fat" (though, according to others, that "fat" may not be easy to see). Breasts or buttocks may be considered by their owners to be either too large or too small. Men, too, are nervous about displaying what they consider to be unmuscular arms or legs. They also may be unduly afraid of not doing everything "right" and of subsequently being corrected in front of the rest of the class.

Self-Revelation

Which is more intimidating—creativity or self-revelation?

I believe it is the latter. Creativity still has the aspect of being under one's control. But revelation? That is indeed impromptu, and unplanned movements do "betray" us.

Many adults who otherwise would love to move stay away from creative movement class because of a question that is answered before the individual shows up to ask it: "What am I going to reveal about myself through my unguarded movement?"

Within the questioner's own mind the answer is stultifying and guilt provoking. Whatever concept we have of improvisation, we all know that "doing one's own movement" means we cannot escape as one may when being taught specific formal exercises by a teacher who watches to see that every finger and toe are placed correctly.

It is the very essence of improvisation that it does reveal us, to ourselves and to all who observe us; we do "give ourselves away." People fear the "evil that lurks within" will be out of hiding, and the "naked truth" will be revealed. This causes paralysis!

Be not paralyzed. Be of good cheer.

The entire emphasis of an improvisation session is to take the fear out of moving and to change it to ease—even in allowing the fears to come through in movement.

The very first comment a newcomer makes to me after the introductory class is an expression of surprise and gratitude, telling me how "comfortable" we made him feel.

This comfort is the key that unlocks the ability to move freely. It is discussed at length under the topic heading of "How to Create Emotional Safety" (see p. 59).

As I work with the body and open up the body to dancing, there's no question about the beauty of the body and the experience all combined. I think my body is beautiful now. And it's great to hear myself say that, because before I was somewhere in the middle. If someone paid me a compliment, I would be like, what are you talking about? And half of me would be accepting but not totally believing, but more and more I'm believing.

I think I've viewed my body up until very recently as a tool to manipulate—as opposed to the shell that I'm living in that's really part of me, like my house.

I was called plump nicknames, but it was affectionately used. It wasn't a big problem. At that time I was part of a Jewish youth group and doing that kind of folk dancing. I always enjoyed the energetic, constantly moving type of dancing. So I don't know how I felt about my body then, but I feel wonderful about it now.

What makes me comfortable, what I like about our classes, is seeing people of so many different shapes, weights, sizes, and proportions all moving in their own styles.

Freedom From Fear

I love the quote about freedom from one of the great English poets, C. Day Lewis: "Freedom is rooted yet unconfined."

Yes, the rootedness is in all the measures we take to provide safety: a nonthreatening ambience, warm group receptivity, a noncritical teacher. We take away the abrasive factors, relieve the mind of worry, ease the tensions of the day so that we can center upon what is as yet unexpressed. Then comes the unconfining; repressed movements being given breath, peeping from under cover, without fear or guilt. Only then are we able to move with full flourish.

Rootedness is part of all freedom; the uprooted are not free but lost. We grow from our roots, and therefore what nourishes our roots is good for us. This nourishment permits us to define ourselves as we grow. Freedom of movement is something that can be learned from lesson to lesson, and we see the exciting growth of freedom before our eyes in every class. Experimentation, daring, and risk-taking are some of the attributes that expand. In addition, greater ease in relating to one's own body and the bodies of others emerges. Ease in relating to other personalities also occurs.

The most wonderful aspect of improvisation is the freedom of group interrelatedness. It is impossible to force people in a group to move in relation to one another. This kind of communication cannot have one false note; it has to be genuine, caring, observant, mutually appreciative, and engaged in by all. These attributes of improv are tastes of the kind of freedom we could be living in all of our lives. Or, as Dina sighed, "Why can't life 'outside' be like this?"

Maria, for whom touching someone else's body has sexual taboos, told me she enjoyed the touching that goes on in group or duo/trio improvs because "it is an approved situation, it is safe, it is within an art context," and she "physically and emotionally enjoys this touching that I could not do otherwise."

I have a lot of hang-ups about my body and my body image. Sometimes I don't come to class because I just feel too fat. Because dancers are always sleek and slender and their ribs stick out. But this is one of the few classes where there are people of all shapes and sizes. I'm always so impressed when someone like Amanda, who is large, moves gently and gracefully and lightly. When she moves, it puts that whole idea of body image in much greater perspective.

When I feel heavy I feel like a butterball and don't feel graceful, but I see other people and see the beauty in the way they move, regardless of whether or not they fit the typical American standard.

All freedom goes through many stages, the first being the recognition of it, and then freedom-*from* to freedom-to. In improv class one can see, in microcosm, the development of freedom. Every human being who walks

A wonderful aspect of improvisation is the freedom of group interrelatedness.

into the studio bears some shackles—physical, social, or emotional. It is not only a body that the person brings, but all the things that body represents to her and to the others viewing her.

Shackles can even come from having had wonderful technical training but no creative training whatsoever. Such was Magda, a mature woman who came to our class from a lifetime of professional ballet abroad, taught in the grand old style. She was used to tights with "feet" and it took a long time for her to expose her bare foot to the floor. (But I have also seen tots who fear taking off their socks to move around in dance class.) The time came when Magda—having gone through stages of fearfulness, strangeness, trust—permitted her entire body to lie on the floor and assume the horizontal position of expressive dance. She had won freedom from the ballet's up-rightness.

The progression of freedoms we have seen happen:

FROM shame of body	TO appreciation for body
FROM dislike of one body part	TO appreciation for that part
FROM shyness in exposing "fat"	TO throwing off the concealing oversize shirt
FROM fear of touching or being touched	TO natural and easy touching
FROM fear of "taking up everybody's time"	TO taking one's own time
FROM fear of competition	TO learning we are all on a creative par

An experienced student: *All those feelings—the fear of looking silly, of being vacuous and being too revealing—I don't connect with those feelings at all any more. I hardly even remember them. I don't know how long it takes to get over it, but I don't see improvisation in those terms any more, and anybody can grow into that.*

Antistress

One would assume that professional dancers use every possible joint and muscle in their bodies, but actually they use only those in the specific "technique" of a particular group's choreographer.

In contrast to this, the improviser uses the entire body, perfecting her movements for herself. This assures that she experiences every personal nuance. We all glimpse the different workouts of the diverse people in the group and become aware of how many millions of movements there are.

Improv gives people another vocabulary—a lexicon of movement with which to describe and feel the stuff of their lives. It is indeed a kind of physical and emotional folklore. The more "words" we know the more we can express; the more we express, the larger our vocabulary becomes.

Observing each student developing a personal, harmonious movement vocabulary has caused me to think of stress as anything that goes against our natural flow. Improv relieves stress by loosening limbs and tension. Improv counters burnout by freeing the body from being locked into its everyday ruts. There is openness and boldness in experimentation and an appetite for further adventurousness. There is increasing physical control: strength, balance, and endurance.

In relation to health this means that the improviser explores only the personal range that a particular body is capable of and desires. There are no stresses or strains resulting from accommodating the demands of someone else's technique. The improviser's self-created exercises are harmonious to him and do not go against his personal grain in any stressful way.

One might ask, if improvisation is extemporaneous and spur-of-the-moment, does it have to be practiced? Although it is spontaneous and natural, to develop and deepen skills takes patience, assurance, and conviction that lengthier expressions will come from small, short spurts of movement. Development is slow and deep.

The teacher and student must keep in mind that one builds skill, endurance, confidence from lesson to lesson. These are qualities bred only by time; they cannot be acquired instantly or superficially. Group rapport is like the consistency of a rich soup that requires lots of stirring and simmering to allow the herbs and flavors to blend.

Just Moving!

One of the greatest things about improvisation is that it gives one "instant satisfaction," the satisfaction of having created and participated in a finished product. It is not merely a "means toward an end," it *is* the end. The end product of improvisation is the only product. It is complete in itself. It doesn't have to be rehearsed or repeated. As a student summed up succinctly: "It is what it is." In fact, an improvisation could not possibly be repeated unless it was videotaped or recorded in some way and then practiced over and over again. It would still lack, however, the delicate but strengthening interplay of classmate and audience that is, after all, the sine qua non of group improvisation.

Even the youngest child who awakens to an art form can make a serious personal commitment. The first lesson learned is that to study at all is to study in earnest. The very process of learning to walk, with the body making its own efforts to go from crawling to toddling to unaided walking, can be an early inspiration for future performances. Yes, this young child is capable of assuming a lifelong discipline. One can impose upon oneself even at the tenderest age a doggedness of practice toward a desired artistry.

The same applies in adulthood. I remind beginner adults who come once a week that just bringing their body to class regularly—especially when they are new to the process—will provide a continuity of experience. In the same miraculous way in which we learn anything, the mind and body retain what they learn and thus we improve our balance, strength, endurance, and control.

PART III

How to Teach Movement Improvisation

What, in the long run, are creative movement classes all about? It is the pupil who is the explorer, while the teacher is only the stimulator. The pupil becomes the active initiator of personal style and specific subject matter instead of copying or interpreting what anyone else may have in mind.

Classes are for people to move, to use their "muscle memories" to do movement that is expressive and individual while at times blending what is theirs with the movement of others.

What follows is about the means used to awaken and reawaken movement. The purpose of this awakening is to call the whole body into play and use it to its utmost, giving the human being a glimpse of that body's physical and emotional capabilities. The challenge is to find every way of making everyday movement visible, important, and enhanced. The movements of life include the internal movement that keeps the blood racing and the organs functioning, as well as other movements like locomotion, feeding, clothing, satisfying bodily needs, and self-protection. When we study improvisation, we take the simplest gesture and give it free play, nurturing and developing it. In a way we can be said to be recapturing the natural. But we are also developing lifelong skills. The individual child or adult who consciously practices this exploration within a group setting learns three advanced non-verbal lessons simultaneously:

- How to produce personal movements
- How to relate one's movements to the movements of others
- How to sense the movement and meaning of the group as a whole

What Does a Teacher Teach?

What are we doing when we teach improvisation? If improvised movement is a form of physical activity that does not require any training—as we practice the recognition and performance of nonverbal cues our whole lives—then what is there to teach? And if we do teach, what is our goal and what is our role?

What we teach is not movement that comes from us and is to be copied—for movements are as unique as individual life experiences—but how to make movement come forth. The teacher then helps to vary, amplify, extend, and direct this student-produced movement for any number of purposes.

Since improv encompasses the whole range of human expressiveness, our approach can only be determined by a concept so unlimited that it will open to us a variety of apparent and unforeseen goals. This concept is that we, the teachers, do not originate the movement but instead work with what our students create. This concept is the bright and shining lens through which all that passes before us in class is observed.

The Teacher's Guiding Concept: Improv Starts From the Students

All improv comes from the lives, bodies, recollections, and experiences of the individuals and group rather than the desires, craft, or artistic taste of any teacher. A genuine eagerness to see what students themselves bring forth, instead of the need to control, shape, impose, codify, or instruct, motivates the teacher of improv. Start with their movements and develop their abilities. That is all.

The teacher starts with these natural movements and helps students develop their individual styles while at the same time shaping group orientation.

Teaching Is Study

Both teacher and pupils are learners who study improvised movement through practice and observation. If we deeply believe this, then there are no set expectations of "success" to work toward or categories into which students and classes are usually divided. There are no good, better, best or bad, worse, worst improvisers. There are just those of us who have become, through conscious study of ourselves and each other, less inhibited, less limited, and more concentrated. There is no judgmental way of describing our efforts to express through our bodies freely; we are all casting off shackles and glimpsing our growing powers.

Role, Approach, Procedure

In one respect, both teacher and students explore and learn within the same framework. The teacher, however, works toward sharing the principles and vision of the larger concept.

In teaching, we usually pass on what we have learned as well as the manner, attitude, and procedure of those who have taught us. As we deal with the improvisational aspect of human activity, however, there is no subject matter or rigorous procedures to be handed down. The concept alone is our workbook; it defines what we are trying to achieve, and from it we derive our principles.

The Concept—The Overall Idea That Guides Us

Another important principle of movement improvisation is to believe that all people improvise all day and every day in the recognition of and response to nonverbal cues. We have all been recognizing and using uncountable improvised movements beginning with our very birth. This is what we should claim as our rightfully rich human heritage.

The concept that spurs us on is that by resuscitating communicative and emotional expressions we will be able to further our lives in both daily living and in artistic achievement. With every class, therefore, we approach the attainment of three goals: being free, emotionally open, and related.

How to Be Free, Emotionally Open, and Related

In order to guide our students toward these aims, let us first be clear about what these complex aspects of our lives are composed of. Understanding the subtle nature of our goals is the provocative basis for the role, approach, and procedure of teacher and students.

Let us begin with definitions of our concepts:

- *Freedom.* Reclaiming the suppressed body as our partner for life (as alive as we are): becoming alert physically and immediately responsive.
- *Amplified expressiveness.* The ability of the body to move with us emotionally, as in infancy, and to use principles of artistry to enhance the genuine.

- *Relatedness to others.* We are social beings. Relating ourselves to others through keener nonverbal communication removes bars from mutual action and understanding.

Let's go further now, asking ourselves, as teachers, how we will explore these areas.

If we must be free, we must first of all inspire trust and confidence by surrounding ourselves with emotional safety, security, and encouragement. Eliciting movement that is genuine and meaningful from a person who may be resistant, frozen, fearful, or shy requires gentleness and sensitivity with no pushing or coercion. We must try to find ways to tempt, coax, and cajole with quiet encouragement and approval without inhibiting delicate little expressions while they are just forming.

It helps for people to be reminded continually that when they are called on they are free to accept or free not to accept whatever thematic material is offered to them. Banish all talk. Discourage efforts by anyone to comment vocally: to explain, analyze, or interpret. The bodies of observers have to be kept quiet too, so that there is no distraction to the improviser.

Here is where the teacher's skill comes in.

As I introduced earlier (on p. 33), the teacher feels that she is sharing a rich background of study, with expertise in how movements can be extended, enriched, and shaped into an artistic experience. This is the one skill the teacher has that other observers don't. As we teachers watch, we make a mental note that Carla needs more work with her hands, that Ethel needs to release her constant smile, that Earl's movements could be more percussive. We use every kind of ingenuity we possess to amplify these students' abilities. We know techniques that can vary and color movement, expand or contract the way it is produced. Some people are minimal, terse, or understated; others are verbose, prolific, perpetual. The first group needs help in expanding, the latter in becoming succinct.

In theater we know how to shape an improv for a specific purpose, such as how to help an actor rehearse and polish particular sequences until a desired effect is produced. We use our eyes to see, but also to "hear" and "feel" as we watch without any inner thought of how we can rearrange, criticize, approve, or discourage. Instead we learn what help an improviser needs in deleting, extending, or varying.

We are on an unending search for techniques that open even further the range of expression and communication. Our sensitivities are alert to the students' needs so that we can suggest appropriate themes that will strengthen their abilities. When students are improvising in front of me, I "watch" them with my body; that is, I let my eyes convey what they are doing directly to my body and try to feel, in an empathetic way, what they are experiencing or portraying. I do this without guessing what it is all about. We teachers do not have to know; they know, and it's their lives they are moving out.

Principles of Movement Improvisation

Part III continues by giving you practical information about how to teach movement improvisation. I explain what I've learned are the principles of improvisational movement. I also share with you my experience of what activities make class time effective and successful as well as what you can do to build a safe and cohesive group.

Principle #1: Provide a Stimulus

The principle of creating a movement stimulus is as simple as naming something and asking a student to move in relation to it. Here, the person has free rein to experiment, rather than copying given movements as in traditional dance techniques. For instance:

Real

"How many ways can you touch your desk (the floor, the wall, your chair)?" "Look at one of your hands; how do all the fingers of that hand move?" "How many ways can you move your shoulders (knees, elbows, head)?"

Imaginary

"Imagine you have a huge ball (ribbon, magic wand, musical instrument)." "You're a giant; let's see you move." "There is a sparkling light in the middle of your chest; let's see what you do with that light." "Imagine any *thing* in the world—an existing thing or whatever fantastic creation of your own that you can visualize clearly—and move with it." "You're anybody you want to be; move like that person." These exercises require each student to make personal choices. The wise teacher will learn a great deal from what the improviser has selected from his or her own life experience. This practice also begins strengthening imagery and concentration.

Emotional

"How does your body feel when you're cold (warm, hot, tired, hungry, lazy)?" "How does your body move when you're in the water (a snow storm, a rainy downpour, a strong blowy wind, a beautiful sunny day)?" "How do you feel when you're sad (glad, mad, happy, friendly)?" "What does it feel like to be in a small space (a huge space, a crowd, a peaceful place)?"

Movement improvisation requires each student to make personal choices from his or her own life experience.

These questions should all be preceded by the remark, "Don't tell us, just *do* it."

There is one major stimulus you can use when the time and setup seem right. You ask, "Who would like to do something that happened to you today? Just show us how you feel about what happened. Don't tell us, just do it."

Don't be put off by the initial use of understood gesture; there is nothing wrong with pantomime. But within and around that miming, within and around those real, everyday movements, will be an emotional quality that will come out of the person that everyone will appreciate—along with their silence. Keep saying firmly: "No explanations. Just do it." "And no performance; do it for yourself, not for us. We're just going to be here." Enforce strict silence "so that the improviser can concentrate."

Most people like to act for an audience. The "ham" in them will rise. But insist upon silence. If necessary, stop the improv, saying, "Excuse me, Alicia, we know you can't concentrate on what you're doing unless there is complete quiet. So would you mind starting again."

Principle #2: Ensure Privacy

Make it very clear that improvisers don't have to explain to anybody what they're doing. You give them your authority to keep their own privacy, which you and their classmates will respect. This will heighten their courage and teach them the value of going by their own judgment. This may allow them to expose deep secrets that need some kind of airing, and possibly even deeper secrets that they may never before have been able to share in words or with anyone else.

Principle #3: Instill Trust of Student to Self, to Classmates, to Teacher

In the course of relating to any thing or to her own body, the student may have an upsurge of emotion. Having, recognizing, and expressing this emotion in movement is what convinces the student to trust her own freedom. The teacher should recognize and cultivate this growth as one of the greatest benefits of improvising.

The teacher may have been seen as a fact giver, a discipline enforcer, an enemy, or an unreachable authority figure. When the improvisational atmosphere is introduced, however, the teacher is seen in a new light: as a creator of an atmosphere of self-discovery and as a protector of each individual from any form of attack who is respectful of each ego. Best of all, the teacher is seen as a codiscoverer and coadventurer; as someone who takes delight in learning from the pupil as the pupil is supposed to learn from the teacher.

What an incentive that is: to learn from and with this freshly discovered collaborator.

Half of the things I do here I probably would not do as forcefully and as effectively if these people were not here. There is something about knowing we're all doing it together, knowing there's support, knowing the good will be brought out. There's something very motivating about not having to give account if I fall short, and I'm not going to be judged; I'm not going to be put down if I make a fool of myself.

Principle #4: Focus Attention Physically and Mentally

This principle is pivotal. By your nonverbal example, you as the teacher will teach students how to pay quality attention. This attention is genuinely accepting and noncritical as demonstrated by your quiet, nonmoving body.

Physical

This physical attentiveness combined with the obvious interest displayed in your facial concentration is a model for those observing with you. I had one fidgety pupil who used to lie on her side, changing positions frequently when we were viewing a classmate's improv. Gradually, over the weeks, she learned to quiet her body—to sit instead of lie, and view whatever was going on all the way through. From her initial attitude it appeared to me that she was being snobbish, making the obvious nonverbal statement that she was detached and didn't have to abide by the atmosphere the rest of us were immersed in. But she slowly came to be fascinated with and respect the improvs of her classmates. This led to self-revelation as well as she shared more of herself with us.

I knew we had "arrived" when another student of mine, a great talker and analyzer who finally stopped making remarks, said to a newcomer who had to articulate everything on her mind, "We don't do that here!"

Mental

Observing the emotional reactions of their classmates nonjudgmentally, without any verbalized discussion or criticism, will foster objectivity, acceptance, and an expanded comprehension of the wide range of expressivity in your students. The teacher can fan this positive way of viewing each other into a glow of genuine appreciation. Sadly, in this society we are so used to being criticized that it feels like drinking water in a parched desert to receive positive attention.

A note about concentration: The quality of our attention in class is in our whole bearing, in our bodies and faces. This concentration permits improvisers to concentrate on what is in their minds. We have learned that without the ability to concentrate, there can be no improvisation. Concentration means that an idea, theme, image, or feeling can be held in the mind while relevant movements come out of the body. This is basic to the very process of improvisation.

We've seen people grow from not paying attention to others to paying attention. Sometimes the intimate things that come through the movements here are expressed more than with close relationships, or anybody else. You're showing things to each other that you don't show in any other aspect of your life.

Most things that happen between the beginning and the end of an improv are linked with yourself and inside yourself and they really don't have to do with the audience. They have to do with my interior feelings: I keep trying to think of ways to move that would show the things I'm feeling.

Principle #5: Improve Physical Skills

Like anything else that is practiced regularly, improvisers become more and more skilled at what they do. Everything improves: imagination, concentration, endurance, visualization, physical prowess. It is like the expansion of a spoken language: The more the body's nonverbal expressivity is used, the more movement "vocabulary" the improviser acquires. Familiar ways of moving increase in power and meaning; that power permits new ways of moving to enter the student's lexicon.

The response to one simple stimulus the teacher can give is a classic illustration of this principle. The stimulus is, "You're on a tightrope." (You can either "put a net" under it, or say the dramatic words, "There's no net!")

The response might be timid or limited at first; some students might merely put one foot in front of the other. But gradually, with experience over the weeks, they may become more surefooted and free in their creation of other improvs so that the next time they walk the tightrope they may take some backward steps or even do tricks. Thus the improvement of the physical skill of balance will have opened up some further movement vocabulary.

I would suggest that you take time to develop physical abilities in every class. The teacher can simply ask any of the following questions: "Can one of you show us something you can do over and over again? We call this endurance." Or, "Who knows what balance is? Can one of you show us how you balance?" Or, "Is there someone who knows how to turn without getting

Themes such as "Tightrope" help students improve physical skills.

dizzy?" "Can one of you kick very high? Can any of you stand on your hands? Can someone demonstrate a somersault? Who can jump high?"

If the ability is a simple skill like a split, you can suggest it be done in different ways. First it could be done slowly, then accompanied by varied use of the hands, arms, and torso.

A few minutes can be set aside every day for all to practice individual skills, with the explanation that "We are not doing this for competition against each other but against ourselves. Take something you can do, or want to do better, and practice it now so we can see you improve every time you come to class." Thus the teacher sets up an atmosphere in which all can be proud of each individual's growing proficiency.

You can further inspire students by reminding the class that Olympic athletes and professional dancers make efforts each day of their lives to improve skills that have already been publicly recognized as extraordinary.

You can cite the remarkable form of learning that developed break dancing. With constant practice, alone and together, the dancers made up their own specialities and took turns watching each other. Break dancers usually admired and encouraged each other; their goal was to be the best they could be, individually. Street observers were impressed with the riveted and respectful interest the group had for each one of its members.

Respect for skill is approached from the unique point of view of improvisation: It is learned through experimentation rather than through exercises dictated by a teacher or other authority. The ideal exercise comes from movements in one of the improviser's own creations. This movement can then be enhanced by the teacher, who can suggest practicing it with different emotions or tempos.

When an improv consists of only one slight movement, I have the improviser do the movement in a number of variations—fast and slow, high and low, huge and tiny (as described on page 110, "How to Build Upon the Tiny Movement Response").

Always in warm-up at the beginning of class, I am seeking out the spontaneous movement or movements being made. The entire group can practice these movements together, so everyone gets the feel and tempo into their own bones. Then they break away from the unison and take the movements out into space, doing their own interpretations of them.

Often, when "Personal Stuff" is done at the end of class, I call a movement some improviser has done an "essence" movement (because it seems to have contained the essence of what the improviser was striving for) and have everyone, including the improviser (who very often doesn't remember what she has done, being so engrossed), do it together. Then I ask the improviser to expand and extend this movement in every way and have everybody else "go with" her.

If someone has attempted a technical feat in the course of the improv but has only partially achieved it, I will stop class immediately after his improv and have everyone experiment with the skill. If the skill was a specific type of turn, the students discover its elements for themselves. It's marvelous, to me, that they unearth principles I would have taught them in a technique class.

Overriding Principle

When I am asked how to teach improvisation, I start my answer with one word: safety. Most people think that because we are dealing with physical movement I mean physical safety—making sure that we are not hurt and do not hurt others. This safety requires self-conscious attention to the body. People also might think of temperamental safety. This involves restraint of behavior—not letting oneself get out of hand, riled up, or too touchy.

But the most important safety for a budding improviser is emotional safety. She must feel safe to be herself. And, simple as that may sound, we all know that layers and layers have to be uncovered before we can get to some of the most delicate and most cherished subtleties within us—subtleties that may be hidden even from ourselves.

Why does improvisation set itself such a difficult task, when it would be easier to create with technical movement alone on a superficial level? I feel that we should be literally moved by themes that move us emotionally. My years of teaching have taught me how safe we must feel to bring forth these emotional movements and nurture them. The following section details how I have learned to arrange the physical ambience so as to provide nonverbal messages of unobtrusive encouragement.

How to Create Emotional Safety

What do I do to eliminate tension and competitiveness? The answer to this question depends on the class setting.

In a Private Studio

I greet newcomers at the door, invite them to sit on a chair near me, and ask, "Are you nervous? Tell me how you feel about this first class you're going to take."

Most express gratitude that they have been asked to express how they feel; and yes, most *are* nervous. Relatively few answer, "Oh, I'm looking forward to it."

To all newcomers I say, "Maybe I'm not like any other teacher you know. I'm not looking at you to criticize; I'm looking at you with great interest just to see what your body is going to do. I do not judge."

At a Workshop

In this setting, some participants are my students and some are their friends or others who are strangers to me.

I make it a point to go over to each stranger entering the workshop studio and introduce myself by first name, ask who has recommended that they come, and then listen with great attention when they give the inevitable apology, "I'm so rusty!" I reassure them immediately: "Oh, 5 minutes after we start you're going to feel comfortable. Leave that to me; that's my job. Also, my students are very friendly and are glad you're here. You're going to be fine. And remember, there's no 'right' or 'wrong' in improvisation."

And, sure enough, after the workshop is over they all say how comfortable they've felt.

In a Class Where We Are All Strangers

I introduce myself by first name and say, "Let's get into a circle and learn each other's names." Then, before I start, I add, "I know several name games, but if any of you know any others, please tell us so we can learn something new." If anyone in the group responds we use their suggestion. Any name game loosens everyone up.

After laughter has broken the tension and we have learned first names, I make a quick transition. "You all know we can't move unless we warm up. This warm-up we're going to do was devised by me to allow you to do as you wish; you will only do what you can do, and you don't have to push yourself. I don't believe in pain." I may at this point cite injury prevention specialist Judy Alter, who declares in *Surviving Exercise* (Houghton Mifflin, 1990): "Don't do any movement that hurts you." Though many teachers still believe "no pain, no gain," I say, "Just do whatever your body can do. You don't have to know your right from your left, and you don't have to follow anyone's movements but your own."

Then I start with the "Top to Toe" warm-up, using each part of the body from the head down. It begins as all face me and I say, "Let's see how many things you can do with your head; just try all the different ways you can move it. But, everything with the head and neck has to be done slowly. So be careful."

After everyone experiments simultaneously, I divide them with an invisible line down the center of the room and say, "OK, let's watch group A." Then group A watches group B. I comment on the enormous variety of movement—movement they can see in front of their own eyes. Then I teach them something technical about the head and neck which they can learn by following me; it's something simple and I don't spend too much time on it. I just want to give them a taste of "technique." They are always receptive and feel they're learning something from an authority.

Then we go down the shoulders, rib cage, arms, etc. After we have isolated each part I teach them something related to its movement. The second section of "Top to Toe" is "dialogues": They keep changing partners (a way to meet everybody) and do a separate interaction related to each isolated part. We all observe each duo. The third section of "Top to Toe" involves moving in space with that isolated part while group A and B watch each other. By this time everybody is warmed up technically, emotionally, and socially, and ready to take on new risks.

Emotional Safety for Adult Beginners

Some people seek movement improvisation classes in connection with their work in health, human services, or performing arts fields. They may want to avoid burnout in their jobs, improve their teaching, or learn new ways of relating to clients or patients. Others want to engage in a creative or art activity for the first time, or to continue previous training for pleasure, fitness, or general well-being.

As an amateur pursuit, movement improvisation offers another way of tasting dance performance without years of preparatory technical discipline. It offers this pleasure and release even to the adult who is an utter beginner or who hasn't had a dance class since childhood. It offers an audience of classmates. It offers their instant appreciation, because there is no stage to separate you from them; they are right there in front of you and you can sense their attention.

Many people want to dance for pleasure and for the benefits of moving, not to devote their lives exclusively to this art form. So we are seeing more and more dance classes for adult "nondancers," including ballet, which is such a strict discipline that had never been taught for recreation before.

Simone de Beauvoir has remarked that aging is a process for the entire society to learn about, prepare for, and participate in from infancy. This should be true of dance too: a dancing society from birth!

The Novice

All who enter an improvisation class for the first time are "beginners" in creative movement. Those who have had some form of movement class in the near or distant past—ballet, tap, gymnastics, physical education, modern dance—are, to me, "renewers."

But there are also newcomers who have had no formal movement training whatever. Novices are especially timid, wary, self-conscious, fearful of being exposed both physically and emotionally, and uncomfortable at being in an underdressed state in unfamiliar surroundings in front of a teacher and other strangers. The transition from being fully clothed to emerging in a leotard or other form-fitting outfit requires daring. New adult students should always be told they can wear "anything comfortable that you can move around in and lie on the floor without being constrained." The relentless scrutiny of the media and of society is such that there seems to be no rescue from the presentation of one's physique to public view. Not only is the body revealed in class—with all its supposed flaws—but one is barefoot, also a most intimate and informal condition.

How does one go about introducing improvisation to such fearful newcomers who have never "moved"—and certainly have never moved "creatively"—before? These same persons may be highly functional in other aspects of life but actually ashamed of body freedom. No matter how safe the atmosphere, the novice has to be made especially welcome.

When you're a newcomer, you see that the rest of the group also has to do what you're doing. They're also called upon to move, and they're also called upon to overcome the same fears you have. So in that sense there's a leveling process. There has to be, otherwise I don't think people would be successful in this kind of situation.

"Everyday" Creativity

As teacher, you begin to relate to these students by taking the attitude that they are constantly moving innovatively whether or not they are aware of it. In the broad sense of the term, everyday responses are creative in that each of us copes with an enormous range of obstacles and finds our own means of overcoming them as they arise. In the course of life, we all cope with people whose random movements we do not understand and with inanimate things both stationary and in motion. We create solutions immediately and nonverbally from both learned behavior and individual variations. Sometimes we use "blinders" to cope with a small part of a larger obstacle: In an onrushing crowd we can make our way quickly by passing through the spaces between people and ignoring impediments themselves.

Speech to All First-Timers

I say, "Now I'm going to give my little speech to newcomers. My speech is that there's no way to begin except to begin. We have all been beginners at some time, and we know what it is like. In this class there is no competition; we all help you do what you want to do."

Sometimes I add: "If you have only known teachers who were there to criticize and test you, I am not one of those. I'm looking at you—if you can believe it—uncritically. I'm not looking at you to see if what you do is right or wrong; there is no right or wrong in creativity. I am looking at you to see what you want to do and how I and all of us can help you do it."

Additional words, when appropriate in dance technique class, are: "Throw away everything you have learned in school about the 'sin' of copying. Here, in this class, we copy. Copy, copy, copy those around you when you need to get a step and you are faltering. Don't try with your mind to copy; try with your eye. Let your eye be riveted to the body you see doing something well, and try to reproduce what that person is doing without thinking of how you should do it; just set up a line between your eye and the body you are copying. This is the way we learn movement. Of course it helps to know what you are doing, and every question will be answered by me as well as I am able. But copying will give you a good eye. The purpose of copying, in improvisation class, is to widen your own experience of movement by getting into the bodies of other movers."

Warm-up

While the experienced students are already pursuing their own personal warm-ups, I stand on the floor with the newcomer and quietly and privately explain to him what they are doing. (See p. 75, "Exploration Warm-up.") I make it brief and simple: "Think of your body as the instrument through which you are used to expressing your feelings and communications with others. What we're doing here is warming up that instrument by moving it as if you're discovering it for the first time. See what it does. Don't attempt any exercises; just go exploring. There's no special way; whatever you do will be fine." Throughout both the warm-up and the rest of class, the nonverbal message the new student should get from your behavior is that we're all here for a session of discovery and are therefore all equals.

I like going out on the floor with my classmates and quietly, separately, focusing in on how I feel, on what muscles need working; stretching, walking, lying on the floor, using the barre. It gets me slowly out of the day I've had and into what my body needs at the moment: Movements that make me feel relaxed, energetic, open.

Whenever there's a semistressful situation, I tend to over-react, questioning my competence, worrying about screwing up. But the warm way the group was assembling made me feel comfortable and reasonably self-assured. When we started to warm up, focusing on my body was just what I needed to do.

First Theme

The first improv is always the same for the beginner:

"Be a melting icicle or candle. Make a choice of one of these and keep it firmly in your mind. Start very tall with arms way overhead, and melt all the way down."

This works with child or adult, man or woman, beginner or professional. Visualizing the "melting" keeps the student's mind's eye busy. "Melting all the way down into a puddle" (of wax or water) ends with the student close to, or spread out on, the floor. There lies utter safety. Beginners who are fearful often get only as far as a crouch; spreading one's body out completely on the floor is as yet too much openness for some to risk. Starting with this most elementary theme, the insecurity the beginner may have arrived in class with also begins to "melt." Fear turns to delighted surprise at how easy it was to produce a beautiful spontaneous sequence.

What Is Learned

This exercise is a powerful instructional experience. It starts the novice on the path of learning that movement is not just exercise (I call dance "informed movement") but a means of coordinating image, body, emotional expression, and group relatedness. The beginner also gets a glimpse of how previous technical study can be related to imagery. The sequence of melting comes out of each student's own visualization.

With the rest of the group as audience, I call first upon those who are new to class. Thus it is obvious that this exercise does not require any previous training. The newcomers choose their own place on the floor and do their improvs simultaneously. I wait until all have melted as far down as they can. When they all rise, there is always a sense of accomplishment, a tiny triumph.

Now, as audience for the more experienced members of class, the newcomers can observe freely—free from tension and intimidation and free of their former fears. They are now open to observing the many different varieties of melting.

When I now choose two or three to melt together (this does not mean they have to touch; just that they are aware of each other), beginner and

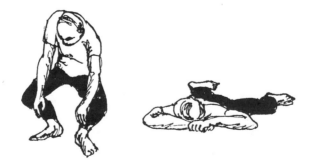

The productive first theme for any beginner is "Be a melting icicle or candle."

experienced are paired together giving a taste and preview of the group interrelatedness that is to come. (For "Icicle/Candle," see Theme #76.)

The Shy and the Show-Off

As children we love to be observed; in fact, we demand it. As adults we also love attention and praise. But if receiving attention involves solo movement in front of others, many adults are embarrassed and shy, and when complimented, may react with disbelief and cynicism. These adults remain self-conscious until, after time, experience, trust, and confidence, they start to enjoy freedom from their inhibitions.

To be utterly frank, there is no possible way to assess how long it takes individuals to gain what we call "trust and confidence." After all, these attributes grow incrementally, subtly, and unevenly. A student may experience a surge of confidence that subsides. Sometimes trust will blossom as a result of one thing someone may say, one especially charged nonverbal interaction, or a powerfully revealing improv one has done or watched.

At the other extreme are those who love to exhibit before others. When these students receive the concentrated, genuine, respectful attention of the group, it helps satisfy them as "performers" and lends an added calm and profundity to their own movement explorations.

These "show-offs" generally come from backgrounds where they had to fight for center stage. In class, having achieved the security of quiet, massive, riveted, accepting attention, they can go more deeply into their own movement expression without searching for social approval of every single movement. What a relief this must be to them! Alas, there are always some who remain unappeased in their need to "milk" (make conscious efforts to arouse) every audience. (See the discussion of shifting roles on pp. 66-67.)

End of First Class

I have learned not only what to say as opening words, but also what to say at the end of class to beginners, who need to hear "how they've done." I take the newcomer aside and ask, "How do you feel you did?" That gives her a chance to articulate thoughts immediately instead of harboring them silently.

I accept whatever she says and then offer my own judgment. I do this very honestly. I never say anything just to make people feel good. I've learned that there is a lot of cynicism about teachers because of experiences with those who give commercial "strokes" or false encouragement.

What I do say is something specific that the student can focus on, like "You have very good balance," or "You did a lovely series of movements in that particular improv" or "You seem to enjoy your creativity" or "You interact very well with others." Or, simply and admiringly, I tell him "You just love to move, don't you?"

Because of this distrust of the traditional teacher, we have a tradition for the student who is having a first class with us: At the end of class, just before dressing or just after everyone has dressed, I say to the newcomer, "We have a tradition here. Your classmates are going to give you their comments. Don't get uptight; they are going to tell you something they liked about what you did; something specific and always positive. Try to listen and accept these compliments. The rest of the world is so busy giving us negative feedback that it takes a little adjusting here to listen to the positive.

"Then you can say something—but only if you want to—to your classmates about how you felt about yourself or them in the class."

There are reasons for traditions; we all enjoy this one.

One of the things I like especially at the beginning was really just going through the various stretches in a kind of disciplined way. And also the way you helped us position various body parts in ways I might not have thought of otherwise. Simple things, like changing the position of the elbow and arm. They're not normal positions that we get into, so it really kind of opens up your mind to experiment with these different positions.

It's really sensitizing me about how much you can get from fairly simple things. Like the kinds of emotions that can be conveyed depending on where your hand is positioned and whether it's held open, palm upward, or palm facing something. You get very different feelings out of it.

Shifting Roles: Classmates as Audience

Though sharing the same purpose can bring any group together, an even deeper and more subtle factor helps knit the improv group's fabric. Within a group that becomes used to sharing its experience nonverbally, all the delicate threads of feeling gradually form an invisible but strongly bonding net. Alternate roles of giving and receiving wordless confidences, of watching and being watched in all emotional moods, make a cohesive group out of any improv class.

In the intimate confines of our classroom, while the students are improvising, improvisers are assured of the constancy of their audience. There is neither applause nor verbal comment. There is, in fact, no usual feedback to the performers whether they are liked or disliked or whether the performance is a "success" or a "failure." What improvisers get from the attentive group of which they are a part is stable, consistent, and unvarying. It is a sameness of focus that can be felt before and during every improv. It is always present and supportive. This very specialized attention nurtures the growth of each student's creative offerings and, in time, is taken for granted as is anything that can be felt as solid, secure, and unvarying.

When I do something by myself in front of the group, it is very supportive and encouraging. When we do something together as a group, it's sharing an experience with the group. I feel very comfortable doing improv with the others because it's relating to somebody else. I've always been concerned about other people and how they feel.

In our improv group I felt safe to take chances and risks. I always feel supported and completely accepted. Thanks for helping me to open and explore within our group atmosphere.

When an improviser is truly focused, the group can watch for a long time, engrossed in what is happening, knowing no explanation is or will be asked.

It's gratifying that people pay attention to what I am doing respectfully and interact with me only as they feel they want to. There's no feeling of doing a performance, of being separate and apart from an audience, because the group atmosphere is totally noncritical.

An actor: *I remember this as a special experience from one of our improv classes. We were to stand individually before the class. That was all. I took this to mean that the class was to silently accept our physical presence; that the whole idea was to make that person, for those few moments, feel that her body/self was totally acknowledged and accepted in that space. Though this experience was only brief, I was able to carry the positive feeling it gave me back out into the street after class time, and I'm thinking about it now.*

Physical Aspects of the Atmosphere

The physical appearance of the room the students enter is not their main concern. They are far too worried about themselves: how they will look and what impression they will make on both their classmates and the teacher, and how they will conduct themselves in comparison with others. But because humans function on many levels at once, the physical atmosphere also contributes to how safe the students feel. The most important aspect of their surroundings is that there is nothing jarring.

The Room

To the professional or serious dance student, a bare room with barres and mirrors, perhaps one window or exit to a fire escape, and combination of electric or fluorescent lighting and battleship-gray linoleum floor, are familiar and accepted. The serious technical work is paramount and nothing else but the class matters. Dancers and teachers are there for one understood goal: technical practice toward perfection, which is aimed for in every use of the body and monitored in the mirror. But to the improviser, whose main work is to produce feelings, recall the past, and make the present emotionally alive, everything must conspire to provide a nurturing atmosphere.

The physical atmosphere is something which is truly nonverbal. The place should not be off-putting; its message should be nontheatrical and nonprofessional to ensure that they will not be intimidated. The test is not how high the ceiling is, how large the room is, or how appropriate the furnishings are, but how it makes those who enter it feel.

Light

Though too self-conscious or too polite to focus on whether the room is bright or dim, people generally find semibrightness most appropriate. For evening classes I adjust the ceiling lights with a dimmer. I start with the lights at their brightest and, as I turn the dimmer down, say, "Let me know when it's just right for you." This way I can adjust the intensity to the particular class' needs. Also, students know they can ask me to give them the light they need for a mood they want to project in a specific improv.

Students in daytime classes also adjust the flow of sunlight and air into the studio according to their needs. They raise or lower the windows, draw the curtains aside, etc. I always invite them to sense each other's preferences and verbally or nonverbally arrive at a common consent.

Climate

I never keep the air conditioner on during class, especially since improvising requires us to stand aside frequently and observe, and at the end of class to sit and watch what various classmates do. If pupils are not in motion it's important to prevent them from becoming chilled. In extremely hot weather I cool the room before class starts.

Creative Use of All Physical Features

If you have posts in your space, these may be incorporated into the friendliness of the ambience by acknowledging them as the pillars they are and not as barriers. They can be sat against, related to as "corners," or seen as boundaries for solo and group work.

Again, since many movement studios are used for ballet, there will be barres. Examples of the ways I would use the barre in improv are:

"Use the barre as something you want to get away from. Let's see what happens."

"The barre is your anchor. You can go far away from it, stay long away from it, leave and then go back to it."

"Let's see what use you want to make of this barre as a prop."

(See #21 in the "Theme" section.)

Aesthetics

Purses and other important things that cannot be left out of sight should be placed in a specific unobtrusive spot, not be scattered about here and there so as to be distracting. Messiness is displeasing and also contracts the space.

Mirrors

It is conventional for dance classes to have a wall of mirrors so students can see how they look. But mirrors are one thing an improv studio must not have. Spotting one's physical looks in a mirror and glimpsing oneself during

The barre in a studio can be used in many ways in improvisation.

an improvisation are both completely antithetical to the very theory of spontaneous movement. Catching sight of oneself in a mirror is disconcerting to both beginner and the highly skilled. The gaze of the improviser is inward. An improviser concentrates upon a theme and looks outward only enough to be aware of the movements of those with whom one is interrelating.

Improvisers never think of the onlookers as audience, or, in the same way, look at themselves as audience. One is not looking at oneself while one is feeling; instead one is concentrating on the feeling and what it is producing inside. To think of how one is looking to someone else—even to oneself—is a betrayal of that inwardly focused feeling.

We have all seen a child gauge what effect crying has on an observing adult. The moment we see that the child is using tears to gain attention, advantage, or power, is the moment we know that the tears are not genuine. The cause of the tears is secondary to the child's use of its effect. In the same way we know when an improvisation is not genuine and is being done merely for effect.

Floor

The ideal floor is beautiful resilient wood. But you may have to make do with linoleum (hopefully without a pattern) or a rug. In an improv class you can use anything underfoot if you have to, knowing it will just dictate that some themes must be eliminated. However, there are enough stimuli to use no matter what the floor is made of. The very texture of the floor covering is, in fact, the underlying reason for a time-honored and appropriate stimulus: "Your foot is new here; it asks itself, 'What is underneath? Is this a meadow? Pebbles? Glass? A piece of fur?' "

This is excellent for an improviser at any stage, but especially for beginners.

Improvisation Is for Every Time, Everywhere!

When you end up in a small rug-covered room in a hotel where you are teaching for a convention, don't despair. What you learn both as teachers and students is to be creative under any circumstances. After all, this is the life lesson of improvisation. With your nonverbal example of adapting to the immediate surroundings, you are teaching students that we can transform any place with our imagination. Recently I arrived to teach at a space that was locked. What did we do? We used the corridor for our class, piling our coats at one end and remaining dressed in street clothes. The alternative was to cancel class. This way, no one who was present will forget the nonverbal message: Improv is important enough to do wherever and whenever.

Class Procedure

The rationale for this class procedure has grown organically from my work. The sequence provides a physical, creative, and emotional warm-up. "Personal Stuff" serves as a transition to the all-improvisation section that ends the class.

Physical Safety

Before class starts I ask if there is anyone with an injury or sensitive spot we should all be aware of during class so we do not injure it.

If the answer is yes, we all gather around that person (or, in workshop, have her stand in the center of our circle) and give our quiet, caring attention to that particular part. We do this to focus the individual's attention on her own hurt, helping her think about whether it is being taken care of properly, as we know people sometimes tend to go through their day neglecting pains.

The group attention is a mark of genuine interest in honoring that particular injured body part. It is also a reminder to everyone to be careful of that part throughout the class.

Recently, at end-of-class improv time, I suggested to Kendra that she work out her sore shoulder in front of us. We observed her testing that shoulder in all the different movements she could think of that might cause a twinge of pain and then immediately soften that movement. When she seemed to have satisfied her understanding of what had been making the shoulder uncomfortable, she stopped.

Dressed and ready to leave for home, Kendra turned to us with a smile that was delighted, puzzled, and pleased. She said, "It really *does* feel better."

Beginning of Class

In a dance class, where technical exercises are interlaced with individual and group creative movement, pupils have already been warmed up and there is no special physical preparation for the improvisation session. We go right into it in the last half-hour of the class.

But in an all-improv class, whether you intend to work with a few individuals or a large group, with experienced or inexperienced people, with strangers or those who know each other, the session must start with some form of physical warm-up.

Because we are building confidence in the handling of one's own body, the warm-up must be noncompetitive. It should not depend on expectations of technical prowess. It must be surrounded with an air of simplicity and ease as well as laughter and encouragement. This allows us to quickly establish a human level that accommodates the wide variety of life experience in the group.

The movement improvisation warm-up is both physical and creative. The aim is for each individual to move every part of the body from the fingers all the way to the toes, "tuning up the instrument." Each student works privately, concentrating on what his body needs at that particular moment and, one need solved, going on to another.

In workshops where people are just being introduced to improv, I personally conduct a "Top to Toe" warm-up/workout, which is described on p. 60.

For children, I sometimes start with a run-around to tap off their super energy, followed by some exercises led by the teacher. I prefer exercises that spring from the creativity of the children themselves, such as "Let's see all the ways you can reach." Or "You're Jack climbing up the beanstalk."

For all age groups every warm-up includes enough footwork so the feet are ready for any hopping, jumping, or leaping that may take place in the course of class.

Improvisation class procedure consists of the following activities:

1. Warm-up for individual and group
2. Stretching
3. Variations on movements taken from warm-ups: moving in duos, trios, group
4. "Personal Stuff" and themes

Warm-ups

I sit aside and do not lead in warm-ups. The atmosphere immediately shifts to one of independent work emanating from the improvisers themselves.

Over the years, we have experimented with three types of warm-ups as follows:

Circle Warm-up

All form a circle in which each student gets a chance to do what her body needs while the others copy simultaneously.

The warm-up starts by my saying: "Everyone comes from a whole day of doing different things and now we have to make ourselves ready to move freely individually and weld our whole group together. Each body needs some different kind of preparation for movement. So take turns. Each of you do as many movements as your particular body needs, and the whole group will do these with you. Everyone will copy your movement's tempo, rhythm, and quality, exactly as you do it."

This group warm-up has these benefits:

- Working out individual tensions lets each person reduce his day's stresses.

- Copying each other's movements sharpens peripheral vision.

- Following another's tempo and being ready for sudden changes develops quickness of response.

- Observing each other doing different movements gives people cooperative group feeling.

- Trying to copy someone else's motions brings instant group rapport, as each person's needs have been given equal attention.

I had very rigid, dogmatic views about ugly movement or pretty movement or wrong or right; everything was connected with that. It developed ultimately into a great case of self-hate because I did not fit into the perfect physical structure for the technique I chose—for ballet. I really feel that finding this class here is kind of a little bit of a repair shop or remediating so that I didn't have to think; . . . either I was going to be great or I shouldn't dance again.

And I have let go of looking at beginners as being wrong or clumsy. I acknowledge they have limited training and just see their expressiveness. But I don't have the feeling that had been instilled when I was the critic and couldn't enjoy a performance if someone went over on her metatarsals.

There's something happening here that's still in a kind of art form that allows for it to be expressed but also stylized. That's the thing I appreciate. I can go at my own pace here. And I tend to be a dramatic person and use expression; you even valued that and brought it to my attention.

Because of the variation in technical ability among the members of the group, if a student can't copy a movement exactly, it is more important that he stay with the rhythm.

The Circle Warm-up is done in silence. When one person has worked out her own body, the group senses who wants to lead next. This quiet sensing is another aspect of our nonverbal training. The warm-up takes as long as is necessary for each person in the circle to get out their own kinks; they generally don't overdo it. There always seems to be a nonverbal consensus about distributing time evenly among the group members.

The Circle Warm-up allows each body to do the movement it needs while the other students copy.

Solo-Duo Warm-up

I say, "Each person warm up first with whatever your body needs. When you've warmed up enough individually, seek a partner and do exercises together."

These are exercise warm-ups that also help develop awareness of others, skill in copying movements, group welding, and experience in duplicating movements different from one's own.

When I observe everyone in pairs, I call out for a circle to form and the warm-up continues as a Circle Warm-up.

The advantage of this variation is that it accommodates both beginners and professionals.

Exploration Warm-up

This is the exercise we have stayed with the longest because it warms up both the physical body and the creative impulses.

This warm-up has three parts. During the first part, I say to the class, "Warm up by yourself. But this is a very specific kind of warm-up. Look at your body, each time you come to class, as a brand new instrument— something that you haven't seen before—whose capabilities and potential you are just discovering. You want to know how each part works and how your parts work in relation to each other. Use your body as a 'laboratory' and do these Exploration Warm-ups until your whole body has been adequately involved."

Then we move into the second part of the warm-up, where I say, "When you've warmed up sufficiently, 'mirror' with a partner, still working experimentally and using the same principle of exploration. Change and work with another partner, or with a trio."

During these two parts of the warm-up I call out names of individuals or duos I think merit attention, so that those who want to interrupt their own work can observe (throughout it is understood that those who don't want to stop to watch others can continue their own work). After a short observation, all resume what they were doing.

Build in such frequent "watching" time in all your classes so that even "show-offs" among the students will feel they have been paid attention to. I take every opportunity to give students experience in watching and being watched. This gives practice in the noncompetitive manner we develop for us all to move in, and it enhances our appreciation for each other.

When everyone has had several changes of partners, and seems warmed up, I take some movement theme from what has been produced and make it available for group participation. This becomes the third part of Exploration Warm-up.

Although the Circle Warm-up gives everybody a good workout and gets the group spirit going because people are watching each other closely and working together, the Exploration Warm-up warms up the exploratory mechanism as well. This deep absorption with the experimental brings freshness and genuine new movement into play and extends concentration skills.

This Exploration Warm-up has been with us for such a long time and has so fulfilled its promise that, truthfully, the teacher can build—as I often do—the rest of the session around it (being sure that stretches are included and also leaving time for "Personal Stuff" and improvs at the end of the class).

Now that the muscles are warm, we are ready for stretches, an essential and regular feature of every class.

Stretches

All stretches by duo and group are done with the understanding that each person stretches self *and* other. This admonition supports both those who are used to "giving in" and those who may typically dominate others. It reminds the group as a whole that this is a venture for all to benefit from.

Solo Stretches

These can be done individually in place to the impetus, "Slow. Elastic. All kinds of body yawns." They can also be done lying on the floor, on one's back, reaching toward others, accompanied by the reminder, "S-l-o-w-l-y." Each person holds an imaginary rod (or a real one, if desired) and uses that to stretch with.

Duo Stretches

Partners choose each other and hold one or both hands. I explain that this is a stretch that two individuals share: "You stretch yourself—because only you know what stretches your body needs—*and* you stretch your partner. This is partly a physical exercise and partly a sensitivity exercise: You do what you have to do and don't pay more attention to your partner than to yourself, but you also remain sensitive to what your partner needs and give that support. So you are each getting what you need, personally, but also being aware of another person's needs." I can't help a little moralizing about this exercise and usually add, "This is good balance in life: neither requiring all the attention nor giving all the attention and thus depriving yourself of getting it."

If this is done in a small group, there can be a change of partners so different sensitivities can be felt. Also, an interesting and more difficult variation can be done by having partners face each other but *not* hold hands. This nontouch relationship arouses more energy than the hand-clasp one. Another stretch, fairly light and "fun," for duo is "pulling taffy between you."

Stretching with a partner allowed me to get in touch with my own needs for body stretching as well as combining those needs with my partner's needs. Having me experience the feeling of serving myself while simultaneously supporting another's needs.

Trang and I work very well together and I'm getting a lot out of it. I think Trang is too. In some exercises, just approaching each other and coming away, or something like that, you do with one person and then you do it with another and it's a completely different experience.

You get to know another person in a very different way by relating nonverbally. And you couldn't even express it. There could be a certain tension you pick up, like if you're holding or pulling or something like that; one person is tight, one is loose.

With one, you might find you're just really coordinated; just going back and forth from one to the other easily or it might be very tight and still. You might either get a countermove or a rigidity.

Solo stretches can be done in place, to each one's own impetus.

Group Stretch for Entire Group

In group stretch—holding hands all around, either on the floor or standing—the entire group is simultaneously involved in stretching themselves and their classmates by grasping whatever part of the body needs to be held to get such a stretch. A's foot may be pressed against B's thigh; C's hand encircled D's wrist; both of E's hands press against the lower back of F, and so on.

All are moving in slow motion. The tempo is slow so that everyone can be caring and observe how to position her or his own body while also giving someone else a hand or other support. The group keeps moving. We know that all are done stretching when the entire group ceases motion and holds to an approximate (unvoiced) count of 10.

Group Stretch for Small Groups

Groups of four or five hold right hands in the center and all "go" with the pull of anyone who exerts pulling pressure. This pull shifts from one person to another, any way it happens. The puller can draw the entire group across the room or in circles or draw the hands upward or down to the floor. The rest of the group members don't resist but quite the opposite: All go willingly and sensitively in the directions and ways the puller draws them.

In a group stretch, the entire group is involved in stretching themselves and their classmates.

Stretching by the Group

I offer, "Who wants to be stretched by everybody?" to recruit a volunteer. Before we start this necessarily careful activity, I ask if there is any hurt limb or sensitive body part we should be aware of.

The "stretchee" can remain passive and let others use their judgment or can indicate what is needed by the positions he stands or lies in, by shifts in the torso, by manipulating his body to indicate how he wants to be stretched.

The group members swarm about, taking places to adjust to these needs: holding arms, legs, head, feet; placing hands on lower or upper back or neck or shoulders, and so on.

All the time this is going on, I speak reminders: "Please give your loving attention. Work on your classmate with care, and also take care that your own body does not become strained.

"Use your hands purposefully and inquiringly, not just placed uselessly. When you feel a muscle in arm or leg or thigh that is tight, keep the warmth of your hands there to try to make this tightness dissolve."

The stretchee can also become aware of this tightness and visualize its softening.

I continue to caution and to repeat; "Be responsible to yourself and to the one you are stretching and to your other classmates. Don't strain yourself while attending to someone else's needs."

The group stretch is supposed to go on till the stretchee says "thank you." But the luxurious feeling is so relaxing that I usually have to bring it to a close so that someone else can be group-stretched.

The purpose of this exercise is for all to become acquainted with each classmate's unique body and become sensitive to it. The work is taken very seriously by all participants. It is a tender, absorbing, quiet activity.

I'm not used to moving with large groups, so when we were all moving together, I experienced a sense of being part of a giant amoeba. I found it disconcerting, but that's OK; new experiences sometimes affect me that way.

It has been an experience of expressing myself totally; a place where I am valued for both my strengths and vulnerabilities, without judgment. Within the group, I have been able to see myself and gain respect and knowledge for who I am.

Of all the classes I've been to, there's one that stands out in my mind because of its emotional impact more than anything else. The theme you gave us was simply to move and then to be quiet, to hold the position. Dana and Sue and I decided to do that together. We made a circle and each did one movement and held it. We hadn't communicated in words how long this was to go on, but there seemed to be a remarkable energy passing between the three of us and we could have gone on for an hour. Each of us was in her own personal state, and yet we were very much a group. We were all exhausted at the end of it; it was all terribly real. It was almost a perfect balance between being able to share something and yet having it very much your own.

There may be one or two people who are new in session, but on the whole they are people I feel comfortable with. They've seen different aspects of me before. It's my group; I give to them and then they give back. And everyone in our group is supportive of newcomers, because they can relate to when they first came to the group and how they felt.

Moving in Space

Thus far we have worked mostly in place.

Next I change the focus from warm-up, mirroring, and stretching to movements that cover the studio floor and keep people moving broadly.

Standing side by side along the barre on one side of the studio, I call on each student to do an exercise alone across the floor. My suggestions may be for each one to do the same exercise or for each one to do something different.

While watching the warm-ups at the beginning of class, I have selected one or several movements that someone was exploring for everyone to try. Then we can cover the floor with duo, trio, and group variations of these movements done individually or simultaneously. Many choreographic arrangements spring spontaneously out of this.

I may suggest:

"Move around with one part of your body leading."

"Move around shifting the lead from one part of the body to another."

"See how many circles you can make." (I purposely leave the interpretation open for the individual to do body turns or trace circles on the floor with feet and/or hands.)

When traveling through space, across the longest path in the room, the diagonal from one corner to its opposite, I may suggest:

"Take the biggest, deepest lunges you can, all across the diagonal. Lunge in every direction."

"Run from your corner to the center of the floor, do any high jump with knees bent, then continue the run to the opposite corner."

"Come down the diagonal in pairs, alternately stretching toward the corner you're leaving and the corner you're approaching."

Choreographic arrangements spring spontaneously out of suggestions like "Move around with one part of your body leading."

With the group divided on opposite sides of the room: "All slide across the room at the same time, according to your own tempos. You can slide forward or sideways. Continue sliding back and forth across the room. No touching, no collisions."

Or, in lieu of any other stimulus given by you, you can suggest to the group: "Any one of you, please divide the group in any way and tell them what to do together." This gives everyone who wishes a chance to choreograph. The student leader may start people from corners, or establish movements in certain areas of the room, or describe floor plans to be followed. Or, she may suggest free circulation with specific movements that she defines, demonstrates, or leaves to each participant's own devising.

Rhythmic Responses

Percussion instruments are used for dancing all over the world. There are heavy drums, gongs, cymbals, timpani, glockenspiels, and xylophones. Many other rhythm-makers, however, are lightweight enough for an individual to handle while moving.

In our studio we have drums, cymbals, finger cymbals (zills), Indian ankle-and-wrist bells on bracelets, triangles, wood blocks, castanets, maracas, wind chimes, bells of all kinds (with handles and on strings), and cowbells.

There are a variety of ways to use these instruments as accompaniment:

- A soloist can use one instrument by itself, several simultaneously, or several sequentially.

- Duos can relate to each other while each partner plays his own instrument.

- The entire group, each with an individual instrument, can play and move together.

- Everyone in the group can handle the same instrument (such as several playing on the same drum).

- I invite each class member in turn to devise a simple but regular rhythm on a drum or on any other instrument or instruments, to which the rest of the group then moves freely, interpreting the rhythm in individual ways. While that student continues playing the rhythm, I call out "Relate on the accented beat."
  "On the accented beat, make a move toward the center and on all other beats move away from the center."
  Or, "Move *only* on drumbeat (cymbal, bell) and not on the rest of the rhythm phrase."
  (See list of activities to percussion in "Theme" section, pp. 160-161.)

Hands and feet stamping and clapping provide more excellent stimuli for group interaction. A group can pound hands on the floor in unison, catching each other's rhythms, copying each other's rhythms, and introducing new ones.

Or you can suggest, "Move around stamping out a regular rhythm with your feet and we'll see how the whole group can pick up one rhythm and all stay with it."

A little "orchestra" can be made of several clapping hands and snapping fingers while one or two move around stamping their feet in response.

Props

Everything and anything that is at hand can be used as a prop. This is true of the percussion instruments; in addition to their value as sound accompaniment students find them good emotional stimuli. Props include whatever can be handled and can give impetus to technical workouts and exploratory themes. Everything stationary in the room can be used as props, including walls and barres.

Uses

There are three stages that we go through in relation to each prop used, and a fourth which is optional:

1. Use the prop for whatever it *feels* like; that is, get the "heft," use it experimentally to see what it is like in the air, in your hand, or in any other context.

2. Use the prop in every way it suggests itself realistically: A piece of fabric can go around the head, the shoulders, the hips, the waist, and so on. A stick can be a pencil, a baton, a dagger, a water diviner.

3. Use the prop in some way that has meaning for you personally.

4. Put the actual prop away and imagine you have it (this activity is optional).

Criteria for Props

Whether for children or adults, props should be as safe as possible for handling. They should not contain sharp ends or rough or jagged spots. However it is not always certain how safely these objects will be used, so the teacher must be especially alert during prop improv time.

The teacher's collection of props grows, and the same ones can be used over and over again by students, each time in a different way. In my group the understanding has always been that a student who brings a prop to class or workshop cannot use that particular prop. In other words, the prop owner is discouraged from preparing how he or she will use it in an improv. Classmates will be able to use the prop spontaneously.

Props need be neither of the elaborate nor bought variety; I search especially for the most common. These props show that our imagination can take advantage of anything, as children often prove. I am always sure that a strange locale or workshop will haply provide us with a prop belonging to those environs: a mop, a chair or bench, a flower vase, a table, a broom.

Here are some of the things we've got:
— A plastic dropcloth (9 × 12 feet)
— Plastic forms from packing
— Cardboard from grocery store fruit cartons
— Plain brown paper bags and shopping bags
— A long rodlike paper core
— A long metal rod
— Paper cartons from milk or other produce
— 1/8 inches aluminum wire. (I wrap cotton and tape around both ends.)
— Hoops of varying widths, sizes, and colors
— Bamboo sticks, about 14 inches long. I have a dozen of these, and they are very popular. They can be used for their percussive possibilities, while duos use them for striking as in duels.

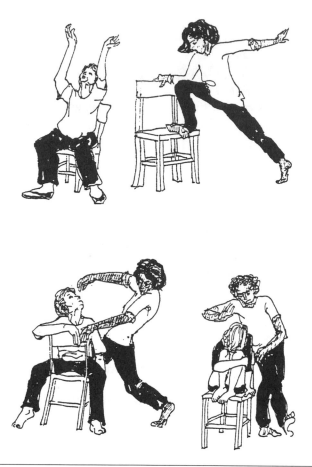

A chair can be a simple and accessible prop that lends itself to many improvisational movements.

— Sugar cane
— A red plastic telephone coil
— A red plastic child's telephone
— A little pillow
— A larger pillow
— Wood blocks light enough to be held in the hand and clicked together by themselves or with a partner's
— A little stool. (Actually, a square crate found on the street, that I covered at one end with a square floor tile for easy sitting. This is one of our most popular studio props.)
— Fabrics: Get one light in color, one black, one bright, one print, one striped, one with bold patterns. There should also be a selection of

textures: lightweight, wool, nubby, patterned, lacelike, velvety. The whole idea is to provide enough difference so students can express whatever they need to.

Also, a bedsheet is good both for solos and for handling by duos and the whole group.

— Found objects: I once found a piece of metal lying in the street that looked like a huge (4-foot) hairpin. It was somewhat chancey from the point of view of safety, but later, entrusted to some highly experienced improvisers—Gregory, Brenda, and June—was used as, among other things, a yoke.

— Ribbons: In every possible color and length and fabric, ribbons provide endless stimulation. Some we can't help calling by the names of those students with whom we most associate their outstanding usages, but those same ribbons are also used by other classmates in entirely different ways. A different ribbon in each student's hand makes for a grand finale. A long, uncut one that all in the group can hold at once takes a lot of communal ingenuity.

When we worked with props, I was immediately drawn to a silky, translucent piece of material—blue/green/purple with a floral design. The improv I did with it had a lot of personal meaning for me. What appealed to me most about the material was softness and femininity, a quality I experience a lot in myself but do not value very highly, judging it as passive, weak, ill defined, lacking in ambition.

I had recently met a man towards whom romantic feelings had developed. In my improv I unfolded the material like a flower opening its petals or unfolding my own desire to love and be loved. Then I billowed it into the air to enjoy its lightness. Then I put it all around me—my head, shoulders, arms. It was very sensual and at the same time protective. I felt a lot of satisfaction in the improv and that I had had the courage to express something about my deepest needs in a very honest way.

A playwright: *We did one improv with masks, and when I got up to do it I had no idea. The warm-ups I had done that day had aroused African responses so I picked a mask because it had stripes in it and I was sort of thinking it looked like zebra stripes. Then I noticed the bamboo stick in the corner of the studio and thought, Well, OK, I'll go to the corner and use the stick—without any idea except that you had given us two different motifs to work on that day in class—of a summoning or a protecting. I hadn't decided between either of them but it became,*

from my point of view, an improv about a tribal personal-
ity in a solitary situation, sort of pulling his powers to-
gether and staking a claim on himself so that he could
sleep for the night.

And that just completely evolved out of itself; it had no
preconception whatsoever. It was a situation in which—
once I grasped the prop—a whole thing developed, and
it had a certain shape and style to it, just because of the
stick itself and the mask.

There was a great deal of strength in all that moving,
and I took chances in swinging the stick around and
luckily remained completely in control. I was even able
to twirl it to a certain degree. That was different, because
I was aware of the degree of technical difficulty right in
the middle of an act of execution in an improvisa-
tional situation.

And Now, to Improvisation Time

After all the technical explorations, stretches, movement in space, use of percussion and props, comes improv time, when we all sit together facing the studio floor.

At this moment there is a subtle shift from warming up to focusing on the product of that warm-up, and a kind of expectancy of what one is going to do as well as what one's classmates are going to produce is tangible. The shift is somewhat like what both audience and musicians experience when the individual instruments have finished tuning up and the attention of all is concentrated on the music to be offered.

It is in this transition from "tuning" the body as an instrument to "playing" on this instrument that the teacher sets a nonverbal example by her conduct, sitting with the others quietly, expectantly. Now is the time for seeing where all this warming up has led us.

It is worth taking note here, again, that along with this expunging of criticism in attitude is a complete lack of criticism in word. The more nonverbal the atmosphere the greater the freedom of physical and emotional expressiveness. In the improv class there must be no discussion, interpretation, challenge, comparison, questioning, or clarification. The improvisation is offered and received. That is all. Whatever has been communicated may be taken differently by each of the observers, but it is taken in silence. (See "Giving 'Reinforcement,' " p. 90.)

"Personal Stuff"

We always start our improv session in a way that may be just personal with us. To new people I explain the derivation of this custom: A student once had a bad experience on her way to class. She came in very distressed saying, "I don't want to talk about it, but can I work out how I feel before we start?"

Of course we all sat as supportive audience and watched her move out those feelings about the incident, and when she had finished and volunteered how much better this had made her feel, we respected her nonverbal communication and didn't probe further.

Thereafter we instituted the "Personal Stuff" time. This can be used by anyone who wants to put into movement something from the day's, week's, or even month's events that has been in their head or inhibiting their muscles. This clears the atmosphere for them before the regular improv session begins.

I introduce this section of class by asking, "Anyone have any 'Personal Stuff?"

Thus, instead of a theme suggested by me, it is one that comes from whatever is uppermost in the student's mind. The theme comes from the very life she is leading. For instance, Sun Mi comes in tired from all the responsibilities of her new baby. She moves this out in front of us while we respectfully watch. After working out her frustrations through her body's movements she's ready to turn her freshened attention to further participation with other classmates.

There is an atmosphere of concentration, inspiration, safety, and creativity in the class. You get more and more involved so that you are able to get to things that bother you through what you do with movement.

In "Personal Stuff" time, I relate this creativity to what I would want to do outside of class: to make decisions, get down to what I really want to do in my life.

Another memorable improv came from one of my own "Personal Stuff." It just so happened that I found a place in the room that became my safe spot—my center—and I found myself staying in that spot until I felt free enough to go forth from there. I would go out and then retreat to my safe spot until I felt ready to emerge and take a risk—always knowing that the safe spot would be there.

Introduction of Themes

Spoken themes constitute only one kind of stimulus for eliciting movement from both the shy and the willing. Motivation can also come from percussion and other sound, from the silent movement of others, and from the handling of props, to name a few possibilities.

When a theme is offered the student must be receptive to it (otherwise I'll offer another, more acceptable one) and immediately concentrate on it. Then we see what the body will do. No one knows in advance what will happen. There is no planning between the statement of the theme and the working out of it. A planned improv is a contradiction.

I say to the student to whom I offer a theme: "Let your mind do the thinking and your body do the moving. Your mind was made for thinking, your body for moving. Keep something in your mind very clearly and constantly and give your body freedom to see what it 'thinks' and 'remembers.'"

We move from concepts that are elementary to themes that train the imagination and start to sharpen the concentration of the inner eye. Next we work with themes that help technique and quality, and finally with themes that involve emotions. The emotions range from delicate nuance to the dynamic. Sometimes they are explosive, but they are always controlled within the class context.

There are elementary themes that involve emotions too, such as: "Show two different sides of yourself."

Or, for duo: "Show attitudes of combat (without touch)."

GS: *How do you do an improv with someone else?*

Greg: *I usually try to be objective and not try to take the lead unless it's obvious the person who's working with me is a little tentative and would kind of rather I started first. I try to figure out what's going on. It's usually characterized—even without eye contact—in terms of dynamics and movement. And I try to take it one step beyond to a broad, conceptual basis, in terms of finding what my thematic approach would be to the material if it were to be transmitted to someone else.*

In the category of emotionalism we go all the way from easy themes to "Your life up to now." Each one of my experienced students has used this

"Attitudes of combat" is a good elementary theme that brings out emotions.

theme, and the most amazing thing about it is that each of them has taken 15 minutes—not much more or less—to do it.

Conduct of the Teacher During "Personal Stuff" and Theme Time

Perhaps you will want to participate along with your students in some or every aspect of the improv class session. However, I take the role of facilitator and enricher in addition to observer. Above all, I am a completely absorbed and concentrated watcher.

The only convention I place upon the improviser is this: "Look for your starting position and then hold that position so we know that is where we are to start looking at you; when you end, hold that position so we know it is the ending."

This admonition also applies to duos, trios, quartets, and the whole group when they are moving at once. A group becomes so amazingly attuned this way that the holding of the final position happens almost instantaneously with all of them, and it is an exciting phenomenon in itself to watch an active group stop almost "on a dime" at seemingly the same moment.

The Rare Interruption.   I'd like to say I never interrupt an improv and that I always wait until it comes to a close. But life qualifies our absolutes. I have learned to use my judgment about the time some improvisations take. Overly long ones don't happen often. But when I sense the class becoming restless and the improviser is unaware about movements that are going on interminably, I have discovered a tactful way of handling it.

My saying "Thank you" discreetly signals the end of that improv, and becomes part of that improviser's learning experience in relation to time-taking. It also earns the approval of the patient group, who appreciate an example of how the teacher uses her judgment for the greater good.

A time when I should have intervened but didn't is still unforgettable to me. A mother and her daughter (in her late teens) were doing a theme in which one "sketches" the motionless other. The daughter's pose involved an uncomfortable neck position and I waited respectfully for the mother to terminate the improv, assuming she'd see the possible hurt involved. But she seemed to be prolonging her "sketching" in such a leisurely way that I sensed some murky undercurrent, and this awareness somehow immobilized me. After class, I couldn't forgive myself for not having interfered in a harmful situation, and phoned the daughter. Fortunately she was young enough to overcome the discomfort to her neck, but I always regret my neglect in this instance.

Though something like this happens rarely over the years, what I learned, as a teacher, is that discretion must overrule any rigid stricture; safety and health for all must be the priority under any circumstance.

So, although the general rule is that the improviser chooses when to end the improv, there are times when the teacher's discretion overrides this principle.

Giving "Reinforcement."   After each "Personal Stuff" improvisation, I have developed the tradition of detaining the improviser after the 10-second hold and adding another dimension to that improv. I will ask one, two, or more classmates to join the improviser on the floor, setting up specific positions of each in relation to the improviser and/or asking all to do something specific that I designate. It may involve facing, touching, or moving in a particular technical or emotional way; it may be asking the entire group to "go with" the improviser (follow or relate to him/her); or it may be to have the improviser watch while the group does something in the character of her improv.

It is a large risk on the part of a teacher to add to an already highly charged emotional expression from the individual improviser, but I have a pact with my students. I remind them of it from time to time. "I do not try to understand or guess what your improvisation is about. So please excuse me if I follow your improvisation with something that seems less intense. What I am doing is taking some movement that you have done and using it for artistic purposes. I try to work with the essence of your movements. And if I do make a mistake, I hope you trust my intentions enough to forgive me."

How, in such a high percentage of cases, I'm able to do something artistically with the essence of their emotional content that does not offend them is something I cannot teach. Perhaps you simply have to, as I have, watch for hundreds of hours. There is no textbook that can teach us to become teachers as well as our students do. To spot the expressive essence of movement makes them feel we understand, while their appreciation for our conversion of that essence into an artistic framework makes us feel they understand.

Watch. Watch with eye, with heart, and with aesthetic concept.

Sometimes, if the material is so moving that we all become emotionally caught up in it, such as after Anne has finished her improv, I will say, "Stay, Anne." Then I ask the rest of the group, or as many as want to, to go and take Anne's last movement phrase along with her. I say "Go and stay close to Anne and take her last movement phrase with her. Then follow her in whatever she does, or just relate to or react to whatever she does afterwards."

In this way Anne gets reinforcement and feels better because she has been strengthened by others joining in her own emotion, and the others get to express their empathy in being able to join her and give her their strength of support.

I frequently make an apology during reinforcement time. No matter how often I have stated it before, I say it with all the sincere caring I said it with the first time. When an improv of an obviously deep emotional nature has just ended, I ask the improviser to please remain just where she has finished, and address her: "You all know that I don't try to analyze or guess what your improv is about; 'that way lies madness.' What I'm doing while observing you is catching one or several of your own movements that I think have the essence of what it is you are moving about. I hope and trust it doesn't offend you if I draw something technical from the emotional basis of your moving. This is just an acknowledgment so you know I am dealing not with the entire feeling that touches you so deeply but just with some small glimpse of it. I'm looking for the 'genuine' and I see it in your essential movement. This way, I hope you can make the transition from what has perhaps hurt you or saddened you into the objective realm of our technical interest.

"The use of this one expressive 'essence' movement taken from your improv may just hit the right note; it may, indeed, echo just what you are feeling. But if not, please excuse me, again."

Positive Comments, Yes!   Although talk is discouraged, there is one type of comment that is invited from time to time, if the improv elicits the need on the part of the observers to express their delight in either the material or its execution. This need may well up from classmates wanting to tell the improviser what an advance she is making technically, creatively, or emotionally.

If his classmates seem to be bubbling in their desire to spur him on, we give brief comments of a positive nature that permit him to know that he is growing. Sometimes he may be aware of this growth and sometimes not. So it is our duty (and joy!) to tell him. This advance of the individual is taken by the group as a sign of their collective growth—for as each member grows, so does the group.

So, we may comment, "The use of that turn was novel," or "Your balance was very strong," or "That was an exciting use of your feet against the floor." Instead of "I don't like" or "Don't do that," we say "If you had stretched your arms just a bit further . . ." or "Adding an extra turn would be more effective."

The Conclusion of Class

Here are some ideas we use for ending class:

Teacher's Nonverbal Statement

I grasp the hands of those seated around me and pull them into a standing circle and without explanation start a series of movements that everyone immediately realizes are to be copied. In this way I round the class off with my own statement in movement, giving the members of the class some technical variety after having been seated watching each other so long. I also may introduce some movements that sharpen their ability to follow me in dynamics and quality.

"Postcards"

If one of our members has returned after a long absence or illness, or had a celebration of some kind in her personal life, or if it is the last class before a holiday or break, we make "postcards": I call A out to stand with me and say to the group in front of us, "Let's give A a send-off postcard for the trip he's about to make (or "Let's welcome B back" or "Let's congratulate C on her anniversary") and the group goes into a static "postcard" grouping.

Then I say, "Let's electrify this card," and the whole group, still standing in place, goes into motion, animating the "card."

These are momentary, spontaneous groupings that are fun and appreciated.

End-of-Semester "Appreciation Round"

We all sit around on the floor so we can see each other's faces, and then each individual gets a chance to hear comments about herself from each of the others all around the circle. Thus, everyone gets a chance to appraise all the others articulately and positively. And, everyone gets to hear about herself from many different points of view. I also get to hear the analytical prowess of the group. I learn about how they perceive each other, about their critical faculties, and about some new aspect of each individual that I hadn't thought about before.

In one session, for instance, they loved Brenda's elongated movements, Dina's shortened improvs, Gregory's deep meanings and wonderful sense of line, and Kahlyani's beautifully produced movement phrases. Cynthia said she saw in Zulay the freedom that she herself is striving for. The group also commented on Liz's increasingly serious material that included anger and anguish.

Fingertip Circle

See the "Theme" section for what we call the "Fingertip Circle," in which we all start by touching fingertips with those to the right and left of us.

Or, you could have a simple circle, with joined or unjoined hands, which ends when all stop moving.

Do find a warm group way to part at the end of each class or workshop, a way that will signify closure.

It is traditional for movement classes to end with applause: thanks for the teacher and appreciation for the work students have done themselves.

We applaud ourselves, each other, the teacher, the art of improvisation, the fun we've had, the hard work we've done, the creativity that's come out of us, and the cumulative progress we've made—the whole shebang!

Following a series of other group improvs, class draws to a close. We are drawn to gather hands in a circle and follow the movements Georgette does. Her closing movements are always different each time class is over, and we follow until she says, "End of class!" amid our applause, in which she joins.

And, Finally—

and forever, to teachers: Remember that we are the instrument in helping people do what they want to do, not what we want them to do. I often have an idea in mind when I suggest a theme. Do they do what I imagine they will? No. But then, do they amaze me with their versions? Yes!

How to Build the Group: From Individuals to Entity

Unlike a one-to-one relationship, movement improvisation involves a group. Each person learns through adjustment to each other individual in that group and to the group as a whole. The group may be seen at first as an intimidating unknown. It may be feared as being composed of aloof or elite others. Those others gradually are seen as allies. And finally, as champions.

In one type of group members come voluntarily, ready and prepared to be united. Though adult students may come for a myriad of reasons—to do some exercise, to lose weight, to accompany a friend, to have an aesthetic experience, to embark on a long-deferred project—they are in class because they want to be. They come knowing, or hoping that they will be made welcome, safe, and unified.

When moving with others, there is a special awareness of each other emotionally and physically. When two strangers dance for the first time, they immediately share something about themselves, a quality which does not always hold true in our daily lives.

Out of the Outside Into the Inside

When students—either children or adults—enter the improv study area, the dressing room through which they must pass is only a partial decompression chamber. They come from all the stimuli, stresses, and strife of the home, the school, or the job, still in street clothes. Stripping these off and donning comfortable, nonrestraining outfits for free movement is a partial transition from the outside world. No matter how casual the attire for walking or work or school or play, the removal of shoes and the contact of the bare foot with the floor constitutes, nonverbally, readiness to put both body and mind into another mode. The focus changes to the physical and creative session to come.

As discussed under several other headings in this book, the change from outside (whatever world) to inside (the confines of the studio) is no small matter. Even when students begin their warm-ups, they may not have "arrived."

Trained to center their complete concentration immediately on the body, the heavy atmosphere of some event of the day may still hover over several individuals. When I observe this, I introduce a spoken suggestion into their concentration: "Take some time to arrive here." This hint gives them the cue that better attention can be paid the warming of the body if the pulls and tugs of whatever tensions they have just come from can be released.

Manuel, for instance, has had to drive for 1-1/2 hours from his job to get here, and the traffic has delayed and agitated him. His eyes are glazed and his shoulders are hiked up. Upon the suggestion that he focus his attention on "arriving" completely in the classroom, he can think through the events of the day, tabling those concerns that distract him from the use of his creativity in the atmosphere of the studio. After this mind-clearing, students are more ready to "listen to their bodies."

I go to class with a totally open mind. I do not prepare for it, either mentally or physically. I don't worry about or anticipate what will happen there. I don't plan what I will do.

No matter how tired I am or how little I feel like being active, I go. Experience has taught me I always feel better when I leave class than when I came.

Reestablishing the Group Each Time

No matter how intimate a group or how often it meets, "groupness" has to be reestablished at every session. The process has to be nursed from the beginning of each class; each time the elements that make up a group have to be reassembled.

The basketball team has just come onto the court. The game does not start right away. There is some individual practice; some interplay between fellow members. However close the players are to each other personally, however often they play together or whatever memories they share, the process of warming up is not only a physical one but a reasserting of group feeling. It may happen quickly or slowly, but time must be left for this or the group is not complete.

Steps in Building "Groupness"

The elements for building a group can be found in the answers to two questions:

1. Is each individual ready to relate to others?
2. What is the most appropriate cementing device at this particular session?

I always let the warm-up start first, before I initiate any steps toward getting the group together as a unit. People have differing body clocks for timing their readiness to participate with others. Liz, for instance (at her own request), was never included in the group work until she had done enough of a warm-up to suit herself. She came from a taxing job which required her to give of herself to young children with enormous needs, and she in turn needed time when she arrived in class to turn her focus to herself.

The timing of when various people are ready to join is one of the subtle lessons the teacher must learn over the course of many classes. When one or several are not yet ready to relate in a joint endeavor it makes for a false and ungenuine effort.

The first step in starting to form a group is to take the focus from individuals working independently and kindle a common interest. During warm-up time, I am a very active observer. I look for a movement or series of movements that someone on the floor is doing for himself personally that can be translated into group language. I see Ernesto is doing something of interest (fresh, resourceful, genuine). I say, "Let's watch Ernesto."

This is when the second step begins. Either I say "You can go back to your own explorations now," and we return to the warm-up, or I say "Everybody go with Ernesto" and the class does what Ernesto is doing.

From focusing together, the group now begins to move together with group intent and without individual withholding. One can see the group meld together gradually as all follow Ernesto physically and mentally.

Now we move to the third step: "Take any of Ernesto's movements that you have just done and go out into space, interacting with each other through this movement."

Thus the group is knit together; now everyone is purposefully connected with everyone else. They are fully aware of each other and move around in duos and clusters as do fish in their familiar habitat of the ocean.

Stimuli to Elicit Group Feeling

In the example just given, we saw a sequence of physical change of focus, physical following of a leader, and, finally, physical participation with a creative element added. In addition to physical stimuli, we also elicit group feeling through emotional and relational experiences.

Physical

Another way to use physicality to bring a group together (after the warm-up, of course) is to suggest: "Everybody lie face down on the floor, all fingertips touching. Keep the hands in the center but move the rest of your body any way you want."

This gives an immediate focus to all, drawing attention away from moving individually on their explorations. It is, as yet, a partial commitment: All are relating to the same center, where their fingers are touching those of others, but each body is still using the rest of itself to move as the individual desires.

You can also suggest: "Everybody go to the middle of the floor, and just hold hands. Let's see what happens. Go until you all stop together." (I do not indicate whether they should stand or sit; it is up to them.)

Because we are used to shaking hands with strangers as a first acknowledgment of meeting in our society, it is fairly safe to ask strangers to join hands in this class. The holding of hands and the formation of a circle are both classic symbols not only of meeting and greeting but of the enclosed space that is formed, providing a further element of inclusion and intimacy.

If, however, I judge that anyone in a group might balk at holding hands, finding it either too immediate or too saccharine a gesture, I just suggest that people get together in the center of the room and give them some other stimulus, like, "All of you move in and out of the center in any way you want until you all stop together."

The groups love to look forward to this mutual nonverbal agreement to stop moving. There is something deeply satisfying about all becoming

"Everybody go to the middle of the floor, and just hold hands" is a stimulus that can elicit group feeling.

motionless at the same time and holding that cessation for several moments quietly. This culmination of a group exercise is very relevant to our discussion of group building: The nonverbal consensus to stop the motions they've been engaged in demonstrates that group unity has been achieved.

Emotional

Sometimes, when class starts, one can sense a great disparity in the moods of the individuals in it. The sensitive teacher should not expect to use physical means of unifying when people are only "half there." The disturbing factors have to be brought into focus in order to achieve a wholeness of atmosphere.

In such a situation I might suggest, "Lie on your back and reach with different parts of your body to someone on one side of you or the other, or to anyone else in the room."

There is something about reaching out and away from oneself and toward another human being that has a positive emotional effect. Also, moving in a recumbent position cradles one's body; each individual faces the ceiling while arms, legs, and torso do the moving. This avoids the whole confrontation of one body to another. Confrontation, after all, is direct, and this exercise on the back leaves one free from complete commitment.

I may suggest to each student, one at a time, "Show us how you feel right now. Don't tell us; show us." This is a basic stimulus of improvisation, and is an excellent one. It gets to the real feelings. It gives everyone who does it relief, as it means not having to push down emotions but bringing them to the surface and exposing them to the air. It is one of the best ways to "ex-"press a pressure, allowing it to "ex-"it.

A visitor's first time in our workshop: *From early on in the session I observed a split in myself between how I actually felt (somewhat shy but also interested and happy to be there) and how I wanted to be (clever, "creative," and entertaining). Another student seemed unusually reticient; she was present but hesitated to participate. Georgette found a way to bring the group's attention to her by giving her an opportunity to express through movement her feelings of the moment. This incident helped to reduce the split in myself. I decided from then on to aim at moving honestly from my own feelings rather than trying to be "imaginative."*

Relating

"Relating" is a word that can be used at any time. Even newcomers understand it. Give the group a stimulus like "walk," and they will make paths everywhere in the studio. But add, "Now, relate as you walk" and immediately another atmosphere pervades the room; people are now making eye contact, touching, moving with each other, moving with awareness, and moving with a different purpose than when each was walking alone.

The word "relate" humanizes any exercise. For instance, when a regular drumbeat is played so that people are moving around on their own to it, you can call out, in the midst of this energetic activity, "Relate!" and instantaneous choreographic grouping results.

Once a group is interrelating, all move around seeking free-ranging partnerships; interactions broaden, bringing a variety of persons into contact.

Mirroring

For this form of relating, people have to be ready to face each other directly in pairs. If I am not sure that everybody is prepared emotionally to be part of a duo, I allow the group as a whole to choose their own timing: "When you feel you've warmed up enough, find someone to mirror with."

Thus, students are left free as to when they want to turn their attention to mutually copying movements with a partner. They also become sensitive to whomever else on the floor is ready for a joint venture.

When everybody has chosen partners, I have the group stop and watch one couple at a time do its mirroring. This way the group gets to focus on each partnership individually and all partners get to be seen. This rhythm of active movement followed by resting and watching others seems to have a cumulative friendly effect.

Verbal Encouragement: Positive and Direct!

Though we are in a nonverbal medium, there are times when we make spoken comments. It's a strange phenomenon of our daily lives that we tend to make comments to others rather than directly to the person we're commenting about, even if that comment is highly complimentary.

I have discussed this strange habit with students and we all agree it's better, instead of passing a compliment through the teacher, to address it directly to the one for whom it is meant. But only one type of comment is acceptable: It must be positive and preferably specific. We tell newcomers what's good about what they have done in their first class with us, avoiding the escape of generalization. We start to let them know immediately that we will tell them only the genuine, that we really are watching them, and that we will continue to tell them only what we mean so that they can believe both us and themselves. Positives only, to build our group. There's enough negativity out there already!

Comments from the group have been: "When we worked as partners, you were easy to work with," "You're a risk-taker; it was great that you got up at the beginning of improv time and felt safe enough with us," "When we were doing the mirroring, you caught on right away." But by far the most frequent comment is: "You seem so comfortable, it's as if this weren't your first time with us." This is said with such genuine pleasure and truthfulness that the newcomer always beams.

We all glow when receiving these "strokes." Approval helps to build us—including the teacher. I am perfectly delighted to be told what's good about what I do, and I even ask for it. I also compliment myself openly if I think I have created an unusually fine class or have devised a particularly apt stimulus for an individual student's needs. The class appreciates my enjoyment of my own creativity!

Voicing superlatives for individual improvisations introduces too much competition; my "thank you" after each one is compliment enough. But I don't hesitate to wax eloquent in appreciation of the technical, emotional, or aesthetic accomplishments of group efforts.

A student: *Tonight you asked us to find something not only to be positive about but that we felt we were* great *about. By the time I had finished moving to "great," I was* great: *I got back in touch with the positive parts of myself. It's deeper—the movement; this is what I think is sending me here. I also know that if there's some negative material, I do have the right not to explore it that deeply— because I'm not in a therapeutic contract.*

GS: *Good! you have a perfect right not to.*

GS: *You say you're trying to get over your fears. What can I as a teacher do to unscare you?*

Amit: *You don't scare me; it's what I do to myself. What you do is fine. When you see me doing something that you think is good, you tell me so, and that makes me feel very good. I need that.*

The Most Unifying Principle

Commonality of purpose is one of the most powerful motivating forces in the world. Acting together on one concept is the greatest unifying principle for a group. Any group of people, small or large, is productive when all know what they're doing. To act on a verbal understanding is one thing, but the way our group takes a nonverbal concept and moves together is truly remarkable.

Here's an example from one recent class that moved us to tears: Linda had just finished her improvisation. It bespoke unusually deep need and sadness. There was a pause and then four of her classmates went to her. I wondered how they would all handle this, but in one moment it became obvious that she was letting her body become loose in their caring embrace. In the next moment this embrace had converted into a cradle that gradually

Belonging to an improv group puts one in a larger context than each separate participant.

lifted her, recumbent, off the floor, strong arms still rocking gently as she was held aloft. Then all went back to sitting as audience for the next improv. Nothing was said, but unity was felt.

We've Built It; Now Let's Live in It!

Primary to our pride is the recognition of the power of the group that has been built through the creativity of the people within it. Without the group the individual could be dancing alone at home. (We've tried this and discovered that it's the attention of our classmates that we miss.)

Now that disparate individuals have become a group through the physical movement and emotional expression they've engaged in together, there's an awareness of that great shuttle that weaves back and forth, each member's individual growth making the entire group stronger. As the group grows so do the individuals in it.

To say, "I'm in a movement improvisation class" is one thing; to say "I'm in an improv group" puts one in a context larger than each separate participant.

A group is at the same time a number of people together and an entity within itself. It has its own character, purpose, and history. A group is an amalgamation and amplification of all its individuals.

PART IV

Themes

To this point, I've explained why movement improvisation is important to me, how it can help people in diverse areas of their lives, and how I conduct my classes to ensure a trusting, appreciative, supportive group is built. Now it's time for me to share more information about the themes that are such an important part of my improv classes.

Anyone can invent themes to elicit movement. The teacher's duty is to take the resulting movement and use it to teach—to build on the tiny movement response and help develop it. Beginners and experienced students will respond differently to themes. Choosing the right theme for a specific person requires knowledge and insight. I explain in this part how I handle each of these responsibilities, and then I describe 163 themes and categorize them according to the level of experience an improviser should have to do them; whether they can be the springboard for a solo, duo, trio, quartet, or group improvisation; and the theme category (artistic, emotional, imaginative, societal, or technical).

I hope you will return often to this section of the book. Add your own ideas to it as you develop them.

Introduction

Movement improvisation is physical. Every stimulus the body responds to elicits different kinds of reactions from muscles, limbs, and nerves. Whether the stimulus is a word, a prop, or percussion sounds, I think of the range of stimuli as a bunch of keys. As teachers we use these keys to unlock and free the widest variety of expressiveness of the human body.

First of all, I rarely have a concrete idea in terms of a fixed image. I'll have sort of a concentrated emotional feeling, or a color, or an aura, something like that to concentrate on. And I'll usually get up to do an improv on an impulse and don't have any idea what it's going to lead to.

With me, an improv can begin from physical feedback: shoulder and leg, for instance. Sometimes it's just a toe—and that'll determine a whole move and whole twist, and a turn will come from that toe. But sometimes it'll gain a momentum and will all seem to mean something and take its own direction. Sometimes it'll give me an idea which gets worked out in the course of the improv itself.

The beauty about improvisation is that it becomes a physicalized thing that other people can actually see and relate to. It's very different from the kind of improvs that I'd experienced in acting class, which dealt with words and situations and people.

What Are Themes?

Themes are verbal stimuli for nonverbal activity. Consisting of a word, a phrase, or a concept, themes are just another form of stimulus. They are like a Rorschach test: inkblots, words, and objects are all emotionally charged in different ways for various people and therefore elicit unique responses.

Why Are Themes Important?

There are improvisation classes for both children and adults that rely exclu-‐ sively on music or percussion for stimulation. In the form of improv I have chosen to develop, the guiding line is what students select from their own lives that literally moves them to move. Yes, they can be encouraged into action by the sight or holding of a precious object, by a drumbeat, by a sound. But people think and words are meaningful to us.

Words are on a par with, and not superior to, any other form of stimulus. A ribbon, a rose, a castanet, a downbeat phrase—all of these things can arouse emotion and motion. I encourage students to keep a word or *concept* in mind to see what associative moves come through the body.

The purpose of using themes to call forth immediate physical and emotional reactions is to make the student a freely responsive being whose thoughts, feelings, and actions are all united. When this responsiveness is practiced in relation to other people it expands human communication, empathy, harmony, and understanding.

How Does the Teacher Use Themes?

A theme (like any stimulus) can mean anything the student takes that theme to mean, and the student's interpretation may have no resemblance to what the teacher envisioned. Ridding ourselves of personal reaction to a theme—how *we* would do it—requires restraint, discipline, and total impersonal conduct from us as teachers. We learn in time how fruitless it is to expect students to conform to our notions.

I have become highly skilled in nonexpectation! And this is a skill I learned patiently, over the years, from my students. As I frequently remark to them, with a sigh of wonderment, "When I say *apple* to a dozen of you, I get a dozen different apples, and certainly not the one I may have had in mind." This compliment to their uniqueness and their ingenuity makes them proud. And pride, after all, is another benefit of the improvisation student's increasing sense of self-worth. A seasoned, highly respected teacher of dance confessed to me her amazement that I could restrain myself from having expectations of theme interpretations: "I would find it very difficult not to look for what *I* expected them to do."

To you, dear person who reads this book, I say this: Please practice restraining yourself from expectation. Instead, open your receptivity and look forward to differences, variety, surprises, ideas quite counter to yours or even undreamed by you. I guarantee that you will be richly rewarded with all manner of mind-stretching, mind-boggling, unexpected delights to refresh your working day. (Maybe my lack of expectations is why I have never suffered from "burnout.")

Beginner/Experienced

For the convenience of the teacher, the theme chart that follows indicates themes for beginner students, for experienced students, and for both. You can expect the experienced improviser to be able to visualize immediately, to stay with the visualization in an entirely concentrated fashion, and to be free of the fear of judgment of both teacher and the other onlookers. The experienced improviser is also free to let her visualization suggest every possible allusion, let it lead to associated ideas, or provide a whole train of thought and follow that train without self-consciousness or "playing to the audience."

The experienced improviser already trusts onlookers and teacher to let a development run its course, no matter where that course takes him. He is open to whatever revelations may lie ahead and is prepared to—in many cases, eager to—deal with them when and if they occur. Whereas the beginner improviser may squelch a revelation through fear, or may welcome the revelation and then stop, fearful of where it may lead, the experienced improviser takes risks. Standing up to risks is another skill that arises out of the regular practice of improvisation.

The term beginner here only refers to doing improvisation, not to the level of life experience. It may apply equally to a highly trained dancer or actor and to a lay student who comes to an improv class with no formal training in movement.

I use the word *beginner* to refer to anyone who has not had previous conscious training in improvising. I say "conscious" for we are all improvising movement every day of our lives and take this improvising for granted on an unconscious level. In improv class we raise improvising to a level of awareness.

I say to students who are just starting with me, "You don't need any qualifications other than life. We are all—child or adult, novice or professional—beginners in some form of emotion, depending on our range of experience." There are some mature adults who have never experienced, or experience late in life, what some children have already been taught by experience.

My Criteria for a Beginner Theme

The fundamental qualification for a beginner theme is that it be something familiar or comfortable. It must allay fears rather than threaten or intimidate. It must introduce the ongoing process of using visualization, create concentration, and stimulate the quest for the genuine which will make the beginner into an experienced improviser.

The Fears That We Must Allay

Students fear not being able to do anything, not being able to do anything correctly, not being able to do what the teacher wants, not being able to appear in a favorable light, being revealed as stupid, clumsy, or awkward in front of others, and allowing one's real self to be glimpsed.

The fear of self-revelation is the most secret fear of all, and accounts for people who stay away in droves from creative movement. There seem to be no human beings who don't feel that somewhere lurks a bestial self, a self that—if it slips out unguardedly—will make oneself and everyone who observes ashamed or afraid, and worst of all, rejected. This fear of judgment is one of the deepest fears. Even fear of ineptitude pales beside the terror of self-revelation.

A first-timer in class may reveal that she needs compassion. Unabashed tears may flow when a beginner does her first improv in front of this audience of strangers. But even the beginner improviser knows that her sadness will evoke sympathy in the viewer. No beginner I have ever had in my teaching career has taken the chance of immediately revealing viciousness, selfishness, cruelty, or anything else that would appall or shock, or provoke scorn, dislike, or disapproval. A beginner avoids judgments that make for a withdrawal of sympathy.

One other fear the teacher must be aware of when the beginner relates to other classmates is that of physical contact. It is safest with all beginners, to use the "no touch" rule in order to avoid a possible distaste of familiarity and exceeding the bounds of physical proximity.

To allay the generalized fears of the beginner improviser, I ask, "Shall I give you something to do with a few others?" Sometimes there are several beginner improvisers in class and I say, "How about my giving something to all you newcomers to do together?" I find this is very often acceptable to everybody, especially when I add that releasing phrase, "Of course you don't have to."

Anne: *I have an urge to withdraw if someone just comes up and touches me without my being aware it's going to happen. I think it's kind of someone intruding on my space.*

GS: *Do you want to change that?*

Anne: *Well, yes, I think I would.*

GS: *How do you react to touching, in class?*

Anne: *No problem. In my mind it's already a pre-planned part of the activity, so it's not a surprise to me. It's more a problem in social settings where I'm not sure what kind of physical contact is appropriate with people I'm saying hello and goodbye to. I'm making actually a conscious effort [toward] touching people a little bit more.*

I want to be comfortable with touch. I'm opening myself more and more to touch. I've observed how other students hug a lot and my barrier stands out by contrast.

How to Introduce the Beginner's First Theme

In this technological era, a useful way to explain a theme's use as a stimulus is in terms of a computer. A computer is a machine into which words, data, and subject matter are typed and that has keys that, when pressed, will retrieve those entries so the operator can see them in print. One form of introduction to a beginner who is trying to understand how to use a theme might be: "Let's say your body is a computer; that it remembers all the movements you have ever seen or done in your entire lifetime—movements you may have forgotten or don't know you even possess. Now think of the 'theme' as a button on the computer. You press it (put a word into your mind) to see what comes out. In other terms, everything relevant to the word or words in the theme, phrase, or concept will be suggested by your mind (the button) to your body."

What I Say for the Beginner's Safety.   "These themes I give you are just to get your mind, imagination, and body moving. If you don't like the theme I offer you, just say 'give me another' and I'll give you one that is acceptable to you." "Actually, if you don't want to do anything, you don't have to." (This so immediately frees them that they want to try.)

I also say, "We're not looking at you to criticize or make judgments or comparisons. We're just looking with interest; we have no other thought in mind. We're just giving you our nonjudgmental attention. As for me, your teacher, I haven't the least preconceived idea of what you're going to do any more than you have. The comments we may make at the end of class will be specific and positive."

What I Say Before the Beginner's First Improv.   "Keep the word, thought, or idea in your head and let it come out of your body. You are what you are thinking about. Keep that thing, that concept, in your mind and let something come by itself. I know it's difficult not to think or plan ahead; I've known students to take a year or more to break themselves of this habit. But you may do it more quickly."

But the most important thing I tell the beginner is: "The movement that comes out in response to pressing one of your computer 'keys' may be just a tiny one. That's fine. All we need to have is one movement, no matter how little."

There are some things I've just learned about myself from what I find difficult or easy when I come here. It has to do with too much planning. Especially during the first sessions, as soon as we got to a part where we were to do something expressive, I began planning what I was going to do. That's a particularly challenging part of the class to me, and I still feel some discomfort because I want to plan something. What I do in my profession has to do with planning.

So one of the things I can get here is a reduction in the amount of planning I do. Once I begin thinking of reducing the plans, I do find I'm able to get past the

*planning and to start doing some things. I don't know
how long I really sustain that, but it does go on for at
least a little while. I'm really having my eyes opened to
the world of movement and what's possible.*

*For me, the biggest value of this kind of improvisation is
concentration. It's picking up, thinking of something and
thinking of just that one thing. When I do that I can't
think about the way my body looks.*

   *I know I'm truly concentrating on themes now, and I
don't plan movements like I did. I do whatever I feel is
right, here and now, and it's got to be for this moment
and I can't do it any other way.*

*I like standing up first and then being told what the
theme is. Because you're already up here, so you immediately have to think very quickly and then move. Whereas
if you're just sitting and thinking about the theme, you
might say to yourself, I don't think I can do that.*

*I used to try to figure out what I would do before I would
do it, and now I just take an idea and I let the movement
come—I improvise at the time that I'm doing. I purposely
don't plan it. Whereas in the beginning, I used to think
that I wouldn't be able to do anything unless I knew
what I was going to do before. And that's not true.*

   *So it's basically an idea, just a conceptual thing, and
then I follow it from there. At the beginning I used to
wonder how I would act if I were a wave coming in to
the shore, instead of just doing it.*

GS: *What do you think you have learned so far about
your creativity in movement? Is it like the creativity you
use in your out-of-class life?*

   Amir: *No. Well, I don't know. That's a hard question.
Because I think it opens something up here. I can't say it's
entirely different either. In the beginning I was thinking
about what we were going to do, and then I just stopped
doing that.*

   *I don't really think before I come here about what I'm
going to do.*

   GS: *Oh, good!! You're past that stage of wondering
what you're going to do in class and now you just come
to wonder at what you're doing.*

*When you give us a theme or we have an idea, we just
keep that in our minds and go with it. I was able to do
that tonight: to take the word "new" as a theme, and it
was new. I had never seen it before; it was new!*

A practical note to teachers: If there is no time in your class to view students one at a time, it is suggested that half the class watch the other half. This procedure has its merits, as the beginner does not have to fear being viewed alone. It also gives her the security of being part of a group that is watching.

How to Build Upon the Tiny Movement Response

I find that building upon a mere flicker of movement is the beginning of the student's understanding of how to use that one genuine move as a key to other movements; a key that unlocks yet other associations, other subtleties, and other avenues. I concentrate on that one small move and ask its originator to make it, in turn, as tiny as it can possibly be and then as enormous as it can be. I suggest that she do that little movement high and low, in a soft and then in a strong way; aim it upward and then downward and then toward the four corners of the room; and subject it to as many different rhythms as she can devise, such as alternating between fast and slow tempos. All these variations are done in place. And then, in space, I tell her: Walk with that movement. Run with it. Take it here and there. Turn it in circles. Do it wherever and however.

The beginner, thus learning to make variations from the tiniest of movements, will employ this skill in relation to other movements that come along. He will learn to add not only technical changes but also to open that little gesture to a wide variety of moods: doing it angrily, sadly, happily, coyly, triumphantly, and so on.

How to Build an Exact Copy

Reproducing movement exactly as it is done in our everyday life is a time-honored form of communication. Whether you call it mime, mimicry, or pantomime, it appears in the improvisations of all students at all levels of experience for varying reasons. When the beginner improviser starts out with these highly recognizable motions, it is from the desire to be secure, and that is all to the good; both you and she want to start from such a base. And it is an excellent base to build upon.

When the improv is over, the teacher can express encouragement to try a few variations (as in the tiny movement response) or to take this movement as a starting point for the concepts of stylization and abstraction.

Stylization/Abstraction

Like the little squiggly line on a page that can be recognized as the symbol for "serpent," we take a "real" movement—let's say a student was hugging herself by clasping her body with encircling arms—and change it so that it is still recognizable but not exact. I say, "Instead of clasping the body, how about holding the arms a little away from the body." It is still seen as a hug, but a little something else has been added. The space between the arm and the body has literally added another dimension; it introduces an aesthetic aspect, and the movement becomes less personal, and more objective or abstracted. This actually introduces a new dimension of thought, which we follow up on immediately by having the group break up into duos while I suggest that the couple do as many embraces as they can without touching. As we watch each pair in turn, the beginner immediately sees her clutching hug being transformed from the real into a stylized form. This is a lesson that stays with everyone.

Observing

Since all students in an improvisation class take turns being both improviser and audience, the beginner improviser starts to become a skilled observer from the first time she watches her classmates, an observer in a way specific to our work.

No matter what mind-set, feelings, or habits the beginning observer has outside the studio, in class he watches with genuine interest. That watching is, at its simplest, a basic courtesy and respect.

But, as in all that seems simple, there is a wonderful complexity in watching alternating with doing, in improvisers alternating as audience. The observer knows the classmate is not a candle, but watches to see how that "candle" is melting. The observer shares and goes along with the visualization presented by the improviser. Thus the beginning observer learns two forms of visualization: one, in her own mind, while she is doing the actual improvisation; the other, as an observer of a classmate's "melting."

This is theater in its purest, most elementary form. It is not only the classic "suspension of disbelief" but also *active* participatory observing. It is not only that the beginner observer sees another candle melting, but feels that melting vicariously in her own body: Yes, seeing not an arm but hot tallow sliding downward is evidence of powerful visualization by both viewer and doer.

Observer-as-improviser, improviser-as-observer: Both appreciate the collaboration of role reversal that gives these moments their magic, their attention-riveting effect, their kinetic connection.

Developmental View

An entire group practicing improvisations regularly by day, week, or month will display a remarkable array of uneven development. Some beginners will immediately grasp the emotional content and play it to the hilt. Some themes that we have categorized as technical may turn out to be emotionally charged. We never know until theme and person meet and grapple.

But if I were to plan a demonstration class in how to move from the familiar, unthreatening, and everyday to the deeply emotional, I would select a prop to base this on for clear illustration.

Everyone, from beginner to the most experienced, handles a prop in the same sequence, as described fully in the "Prop" section on pp. 82-86. I'll review the steps with which we handle props to explain developmental stages of response: (1) Handle the prop for the very experience of handling it: for its weight, its length, its texture, and its shape. (2) Now use that prop in every way one would use it in real life: The stick becomes a drumstick, a flute, a pointer, a ruler. (3) Now use that prop in a way that has particular significance to you, yourself. (Here emerges personal or emotional significance, at whatever stage the improviser can relate it to any part of real life.) (4) The "real" prop is no longer in your hands; move "as if" the real prop were (any imaginative thing). You can also follow a similar development with an everyday gesture such as a hand wave or a locomotor movement such as walking.

This series condenses the evolution from a lightly imaginative to the deeply emotional improvisation into one session. This development takes place unevenly in everyone throughout a whole semester.

I remember an improv about a difficulty I was having. After I did it, I sort of stood away from the bad feelings the difficulty had given me and said [laughter], You know, there's something very amusing—something very funny—about somebody else being able to make you feel that bad [laugh]. It changed the way I approached the whole thing. Ever since that particular improv, the difficulty has gotten much easier. It's interesting to remember that that was a few months ago and now I'm not having that problem.

Concentration/Quality Attention

In most public audiences there is shifting of bodies, positions, glances, and gazes throughout a performance. Not so in improv class. As I write this, I suddenly realize not only how motionless we are as audience for our classmates, but how relaxed that motionlessness is. Having stopped to speculate on this phenomenon, I conclude that this is what happens to a body when the mind is as genuinely and actively engaged as ours are. We are concentrating not only out of our own interest in what is in front of us but also because we know that our concentration creates the arena for whatever goes on.

The improvisation process itself is impossible without concentration. If one concentrates on moving like a giant and begins taking giant steps, the merest moment of thinking of oneself as Mary or John will make the body falter. One must recover the giantness again immediately, and remain with it unflaggingly. Thus is concentration practiced: One learns to concentrate for longer and longer periods of time, and from one class to the next.

Only through concentration as both mover and audience can the beginner become an experienced improviser. Concentration, in fact, is the prime prerequisite for being able to give quality attention. In how many places in the "outside" world do we get the undivided and interested attention of others? It is within the aura of a group's complete attention that the beginner first learns what it means to be safe enough to put out those delicate little shoots of self-realization. From there the beginner grows incrementally as classmates watch.

This quality attention is also important for the experienced improviser; she expects it, and therefore goes forth boldly into whatever flights of imagination, feats of daring, or realms of fantasy beckon, knowing our nonjudgmental watching eyes are wise in the range of human emotions.

Kevin: *Any frights or dreads you have beforehand, somehow or other are dissipated when you stop thinking of looking silly, or what they will guess about you as they watch you—because movements are very revealing, especially when they're unguarded. When you gradually start focusing on what you're doing—really focusing—it doesn't matter any more what people see in you. What matters is accomplishing what you've been put into a situation to do.*

So, yes, the fears exist, but they become nonexistent once you become involved in what you're doing.

GS: *Almost every adult who's come to class has had these fears.*

Some Tips to the Teacher About Theme Time

What we're always looking for throughout the exploratory warm-up at the beginning of class, and in every improvisation, is that which is genuine.

The genuine rises from felt emotion, from totally concentrated attention, from the energy of a grasped concept, and from the completely willing participation of others. It is absence of artifice and of searching for attention, admiration, or approval. In the course of our lives, we all recognize the genuine greeting arising from real warmth, the genuine attention arising from real interest, and the genuine caring arising from real affection. As teacher, you will distinguish the genuine from the superficial; the genuine arises from the depths of students' internal workings whereas the superficial rises from nowhere. It is upon genuine movement that we build; building on anything else is shaky and lacks solidity. The emotion that brought forth that original genuine movement is there to be tapped into.

If what teacher and students recognize as being genuine comes from the deep wellspring within us where movement originates, everyone will keep striving, throughout all the improvs they do, to tap this source. That intention can bring forth other expressions that become the basis for a number of artistic, emotional, and technical treatments. Each attempt to reach the genuine will be like the compass quivering until it comes to point at true north.

And what helps to make this happen? The student feeling safe with the teacher's unswerving quality attention.

GS: *Do you have any feelings about the length of your improvs—about whether your improv goes on too long?*

Lita: *I guess I've had a moment or two of embarrassment; every once in a while I say to myself that I must be boring people.*

GS: *Do you hear voices telling you you are boring, or to hurry, or to be in a rush?*

Lita: *Yes, sometimes I hear something like "OK, that's enough" or "Don't overdo it" or "Your idea has run out of steam" or sometimes it just ends because the feeling has ended.*

GS: *We have "art time" here; take time to concentrate on your imagery, your feelings, your life.*

I was always afraid I was using up too much time by my improvs. It was very hard for me to claim much time for myself. So for several years GS and I had a pact that she would secretly devise improvs for me to give me the sense that the time I took up in class was permissible. And by the end of our second year when we had our "go-around" and everybody appraises everybody else, someone said to me, "Oh, I so admire the way you take your time when you're doing improvs!" Georgette and I looked at each other and laughed.

PS from GS: *Occasionally a student and I will agree to concentrate on something specific that needs to be changed, and work on it in class in as many different ways we can. I gladly enter into such an understanding.*

Hold.   As I've said before, the only request I make of improvisers is that they hold the beginning movement of their improv so we know that's where it starts and also hold the end position to an inner count of 10 so we know it's the end. Over time we've learned how powerful that ending position can be when it's held; the holding seems to express the essence of what has been done. Also, a need to recognize and respect a conclusion gives this holding a kind of artistic frame, final flourish, an appropriately acknowledged cessation for this evanescent work we do that I always say is "written on the air but whose texture remains palpable."

"Art Time."   Being patient observers rewards all of us. Those who are initially afraid that they're "taking up too much time" by making their improvs too long learn that we have what I call "art time": That is, the time art takes is the time art takes; there is no other time measure.

Those who are shy, or are used to rushing through life or setting their pace by the emotional watches of others, learn that the time we spend with them as an individual is as important as the time we spend observing anyone else in class. Those classmates who are afraid they're taking too much time learn, through our patient timeless attention, something that they carry over into other areas of their lives. They learn to take whatever time they need to express themselves, and grow in self-respect and in our respect.

With those who are gluttons for attention and want to go on and on, the teacher must use discretion. Say your "thank you" at some likely juncture and they will gradually learn that they don't have to do anything extreme to get your or the class's attention. They will learn to be secure in a lesser rather than an outlandish use of their art time.

Thank You.   I thank by first name every student for his effort—no matter what it has produced. Right after her improv I say "Thank you, Alice." This thank you wells up from my deep appreciation. It is genuine.

GS: *What is the process when I suggest a theme to you? For instance, let's take a theme like "space."*

Greg: *I go completely visual, with eyes closed. First I might project a night sky and stars, and within that I can do anything I want. I can move like a comet tail, I can be a quantum of light, I can be a great mass of burning gas, I can be just blackness and absolutely nothing. The concept of "space" would suggest for me to be expansive, just as a beginning move. But I might go the other way, and begin as a ball on the floor and then expand. I could start in a ball and move on a diagonal, probably, and slowly expand. Find a central position and move sort of around myself with my hands and legs spherically; from there, branch out in a spiral with arms out. And then an enlarging of the spiral, and maybe grabbing different corners of the room to represent different elemental influences, and moving back into the center and out from side to side.*

Mind and body sort of build on each other, one sort of leads to another. It's a curious process.

GS: *How do you work when I give a theme such as nuclear disasters—like when we heard about Love Canal and Three-Mile Island?*

Greg: *I look at it from the broadest conceivable scope of human horror, and I have a vivid imagination. I* *approach something like that very seriously. I tend to look for some sort of broad thematic underlining.*

With Three-Mile Island, there was more of quiet ineffable horror than actual physicalized anger. And that in itself is a kind of statement: beyond anger, absolutely beyond anger.

When something has that degree of direct emotional impact—and I was working with Mary, and obviously it had a great deal of emotional impact with her—that was a situation in which she and I were in a position of relating to each other to begin with, and we just sort of took it from there.

Half the time I couldn't tell what she was doing and I'm sure she couldn't tell what I was doing, but we must both have been very heavily concentrating, concentrating on this horror. And I could feel myself going through a thousand changes, and I'm sure she did too.

For some strange reason I am relatively comfortable about doing an improv of that kind of emotional profundity.

How Are Themes Derived?

The principle underlying the creation of themes for improvisation is simple and utterly functional. Themes come from everyday life. You, the teacher, lead an everyday life—whatever kind of life it may be. Take your themes from that life and you will find an open vista.

What is the key to unlocking millions of themes? It is in knowing what you are looking for. You are looking for words, phrases, and concepts that, when tossed out to a group of students, will light a spark in one or some of them that can get them moving and emotionally expressive. The less specific you are, the better; students' interpretations of stimuli vary so widely that the more ambiguous and open-ended the theme, the greater the possibilities.

May I suggest the following process to you: From the moment you open your eyes in the morning, with every move and motion, ask yourself, "What am I doing? What am I thinking? What associations am I making?" The answers will be your themes.

We will put all themes in bold type during your monologue:

I am **awake**. It is **morning**. It is **daybreak**. There is **light** outside my window. (The word **light** is ambiguous, as well it should be; neither you nor the student know which meaning of **light** is going to be interpreted; the student may use the **light** that is the opposite, not of dark, but of heavy.) Thinking of **light** makes me also think of **darkness**. The window needs to be opened. I might suggest the phrase **open all the windows in the world**. Now I remember I had a **dream**. It really was a **nightmare**. It took me a long time to get to **sleep**. **Sleeplessness**. I had to **toss** and **turn**. **To the right, to the left**. They say that in sleeping we change positions often. **Sleeping positions** or **positions during sleep**. The alarm clock startled me. **Something that startles you**. Now I have to get up and I'm resisting it. **Resistance**. Well, I've just got to get up. **Rising. Rising and descending. Arising. How do you get up in the morning? From lying to sitting. From lying to standing.**

Now I've got to take a shower. **Cold shower. Hot shower. Be any kind of water.** (You may get waterfalls, a river, a stream, a downpour.) **From room to room. Homelessness. Washing.** (Students may wash themselves, or wash clothes, or wash a wall.) **Bathing.** (They may bathe in a stream, a tub, or bathe the dog.) I look at myself in the mirror. **Mirror. See yourself in a mirror or use a partner as your mirror. See a self you like in a mirror. See a self you don't like in a mirror. See a ghost or an apparition. See your resemblance to a parent. Do something you do in the way your parent does it.**

Now to breakfast. **Hunger. Food.** (We once saw an experienced improviser using the word **food** as a theme, and it's quite a memory. She kept shoveling what was obviously foot long pasta into her mouth in a constant, rapid tempo, the strands coming into her mouth from here, from there, from everywhere. She never stopped for an instant and did it all with great studiousness, great concentration, getting more and more tired, more and more compulsive, kneeling, sitting, rolling on the floor. We were all hurting with her, with a recognition and sympathy that she found supportive.

This is an example of how important it was for us, the observers, to withhold our laughter. There was an element of comedy at the beginning of this improv, but it is good we reserved merriment; it was not only *not* funny, but it grew more and more serious as it went on. Had we laughed, the intent of the improviser would have been blighted; she would have had a perfect right not to trust us with her painful situation.

Getting dressed. I used this theme at a workshop once. It was fascinating to all of us to watch the way men and women put on their familiar (imaginary) garments, pulling on bras, garter belts, shorts, shirts, slips, skirts, socks, stockings, shoes, boots, T-shirts, sweaters.

Well, you already have lots of themes and the day has just begun! If you are ever at a loss for a theme, all you have to do is ask the student—beginner or experienced—to do "something from your day: an incident, an emotion, a movement." We are all reminded that improvisation comes from the everyday, from what literally moves us.

Students can always be asked to provide themes for each other. The simplest are "one-word themes." Either anyone in the group can call out a one-word theme for a solo improviser, or everyone in the group can call out words until the solo improviser selects one. Or, one person can provide one word for an entire group to use as an improv.

There's also a group action in which everyone walks around until one person calls out a word descriptive of the walking, and the entire group responds immediately by walking that way. For instance, someone may call out, "tired," and the entire group walks in a "tired" way until someone else calls out something else—it might be a "sad" walk or a "stilts" walk or a "cat" walk.

Confession: What I Cannot Pass Along to You

I do two things in class that I try to share with my students and that I cannot, even with the most experienced of them.

One is how I choose the "right" theme for a student who requests it and the other is how I give "reinforcement." The closest I can come is this advice: Watch for hundreds of hours, paying very close attention to each and every person who moves before your eyes, and then you'll know as much as I can tell.

GS: *What are your ideas about how improvising happens? The body seems to have a great deal more to say than the mind does, because I can find myself feeling and experiencing a successful improv without really being able to tell you what I was thinking about.*

You do it and you do it, and then your body tells you things.

Sometimes my impulse may be the theme you give. Or I don't like it but I'm going to do it anyway; so it's pushing myself with a kind of negative thing. Sometimes the impulse is just to explore the movement itself. And sometimes you get out on the floor with someone you just love moving with.

At the beginning, I was doing improvs without my heart in it, so I was bored and I felt I was boring others. But recently I've felt interested and have become connected with where the movements are going—with the idea. Once I have the idea, the first thing that comes to mind is a starting position. When I think I have that down, I build on movements from there. If I find there's a point where I can't think of anything else, and my body just doesn't seem to move, then it's time for me to end it.

One student writes about her improv with a red ribbon: *My theme was sadness and the red ribbon was symbolic to me of that feeling. I began seated and let the wide ribbon fall in front of my eyes. I followed the ribbon with my head going down and then slowly took each end of the ribbon and stretched it taut in front of my standing body. It is difficult for me to remember the sequence but I had two experiences. The first was that the red ribbon somehow took me over in the movement and it felt like some kind of ritual. The second experience contained moments of intense sorrow mixed with a desperate fear. The ribbon crisscrossed my torso and came up over my mouth tightly. I left it there for a moment, feeling trapped and somehow also feeling my movement and the ribbon would release me—which did happen. The ribbon also led me around in stately walks and, again, I felt part of a ritual. The last movement led into bending my torso backward, holding the ribbon taut between my hands. My mouth felt like a "silent scream."*

Katrina: *I remember my first improv about 5 or 6 years ago; I was just turning 30. The theme was an image of being stuck in [a] quagmire, and I was lying on my back. I thought it would be a struggle, and I started to pull myself up, like there was a rope. I can't describe it; I don't think a lot while I'm moving.*

    GS: *When you pulled yourself up hand over hand, you were doing something technical that you hadn't been able to. But in that improv, you just* lifted *yourself up off the floor and fiercely kept up with the rope, as if there had been a real rope there.*

Organization of Theme Section

The themes that follow are organized into a table for quick access. Each theme has a number, and the name of the theme appears in bold type.

To categorize themes as "elementary and therefore simple" or "advanced and therefore complex," in relation to any particular student is as chancy as anything else having to do with an individual. Things are, indeed, not so simple as we think they "should" be; we saw a humorous concept turned into a horror during the course of the development of one improv. We human beings are full of surprises, and the improv class has a front seat on the deep truths, vicissitudes, and contradictions of life. Therefore, in the table, "Beginner" refers to anyone who has had no previous training in movement improvisation. "Experienced" refers to the improviser who has had enough exposure to movement improvisation to feel safe with the thematic subject proposed.

The abbreviations under the Participants column refer to the number of improvisers for whom the theme is used most successfully. The abbreviations are defined here:

S = Solo   **D = Duo**   **T = Trio**
   Q = Quartet   **G = Group**

The Category column denotes the purpose for which the theme can be used. The categories are abbreviated like this:

& = And   (S & G = solo and group, D & G = duo and group, etc.)

&# = Any   Undefined number of people added, for example, to solo (S & #) or duo (D & #), etc.

Art = Artistic   Lends itself to the art of the dance, or can be seen in aesthetic terms; choreographic.

Emo = Emotional   Has feeling rather than thought content.

Imag = Imaginative   Uses recollection or the inner eye; requires ability to make up something that doesn't exist or for which there's no precedent.

Soc = Societal   Interactive with others.

Tech = Technical   Leads to, or requires, physical ability or skill.

Panto = Pantomime   Copies movements exactly from real life.

Game = Game   Combines playful elements for amusement, with governing rules.

Some themes have additional notes on how that theme came to me or what my students have done with particular thematic material.

Themes

#	Theme	Number of participants		Category
		Beginner	Experienced	
1	**Amoeba.**	S,D		Soc, Tech
2	"Have a partner be your **model** and then			
	A. make a drawing of your model."	D		Art
	B. do a painting of her/him."	D		Art
	C. do a sculpture of him/her."	D		Art
3	A. "Visualize a **structure** and show its outline to us."		S	Art
	B. "Move around in the interior of that structure."		S	Art
	C. "Does anyone want to join in?"		D,T,Q,G	Art
4	"Make a continuous **drawing**."	S		Art
5	**Apart and together.** (It can also be called parting and reuniting, separating and drawing together, alone and together, hello and goodbye, going away from and returning to, in and out).	D,G		Soc
6	Huge **canvas**.			
	A. "Use it in any way (apply brush, crayon, or finger paint)."	S		Art
	B. "You are the painting."	S		Art

7	**Gather and scatter.** Everyone start loosely at outside rim (or corners) of room, then run together and freeze. Next everyone run back to their original places. Continue this sequence: Run together, freeze, return. (Note: Hold freeze until all are gathered together.)	G	Soc
8	"**Arising from sleep,** how do you wake up?"	S	Panto
9	"Let one arm have one **character,** the other arm another character."	S	Tech
10	"**Bodies Don't Tell Lies.**" Words and body movements are contradictory.	S	Game
11	**Balance.**		
	A. A no-contact fight for two: "First one of you is down for the punch, then the other. Go to the floor and back up again with differing speeds; for example, hit the floor and spring back or fall slowly and recover slowly."	D	Tech
	B. Same thing; use variations of falls as you go down.	T,Q,G	Tech
	C. "Balance various imaginary objects on different parts of your body such as your head and nose."	D	Tech
	D. "Go across a stream from one slippery rock to another."	S,D	Soc, Tech

E. "Balance on a high wire."	S,D		Tech
F. "Play on a seesaw with a partner."	D		Soc, Imag, Panto
G. "You are in a boat on the rolling sea."	S	S,D,G	Imag
H. "Work with two things in your life you are trying to balance."		S	Emo
I. "Recall an incident in life that threw you off balance."		S	Emo
J. "Take something from your life that has unbalanced you and bring it into balance."		S	Emo
12 "Find reasons for moving with one part of the body **leading**."	S	S	Tech
13 **Becoming**.			
A. "Be something and then show the stages of becoming the opposite of that thing."		S	Imag
B. "Be something. Then become something else."		S	Imag
C. "Act some way you don't like to be. Then change to the way you would like to act or be."		S	Emo
14 "Perform daring feats of **balance** (use one or two others to help)."	S&#	S&#	Tech
15 **Beginning, middle, end**.		S	Imag
16 "What do you feel about a specific **body part**?"			
A. "Improvise, using it the way you feel about it."		S	Emo

B. "Praise a criticized part of your body by showing off its ability."	S		Emo
C. "Take a body part that feels tight and move it until it's free."	S		Tech
D. "Say an adjective or adverb out loud and improvise the movement it describes for one body part (for example, foot: lively; neck: rubbery; head: droopy)."	S		Tech

17 Praise the **body**.
"Tonight Sal is having trouble with her knee, Dee with her thigh. Let's do 'exalting the body: what it means to us.' "

A. "Praise, in movement, one or more of the different parts of your body."	S		Emo
B. "Praise a 'weak' or 'strong' part of your body."	S		Emo

18 **Bases**.
One person goes in each corner and one in the center. All four run to the next "base" (corner) simultaneously. The one in the center displaces someone at base by getting there first. Then that displaced person becomes the center.

For 5   For 5   Tech

19 **Obstacles**.

A. "Visualize various things on the floor that would impede	S	S	Imag

you. Then move around, over, under, or through them."			
B. "Classmates suggest three obstacles. You visualize where these are on the floor and find ways of evading them in getting from one side of the room to the other."		S	Imag
20 "Make all the extravagant **curtain call bows** you can think of. Your classmates will applaud you wildly after each bow."	S,D,T	S,D,T	Art
21 Holding onto the **barre**.			
A. "The barre represents everything you want to get away from."	S	S	Emo
B. "The barre represents everything familiar and comfortable, no matter where you roam."	S	S	Emo
22 For **confidence**. "Create the world!"		S	Emo, Imag
23 **City life**.			
A. Street crossings.	S,D,T,G	S,D,Q,G	Imag
B. Accident.	S&G	S&G	Imag, Soc, Emo
C. Supermarket.	S&#	S&#	Imag, Panto
D. Fire!		G	Soc, Emo
E. Traffic.	G	G	Soc
F. "React to buildings, tempo, or noise."	S	S	Imag, Panto
24 **Circles**.			
A. "Stand in two circles, one inside the other (with fewer people in the inner one). All slide around the same way."	G	G	Tech

B. "Do the same things but the center circle determines the direction of slides and the outer circle slides in the opposite direction."	G	G	Tech
C. The group sits on the floor in a circle.			
(1) "Describe something in motion. Give it in to center of circle."	G	G	Imag
(2) "One person lays a foundation. Each adds to it, until the structure is completed."	G	G	Imag
(3) "Make something and pass it around for each person to handle and do things with."	G	G	Imag

25 **Contrasts**.

A. Dynamic interplay of contrasts for duo or two groups.

First person or group is:	Second person or group is:
high	low
sharp	smooth
quick	slow

(1) The first group remains high and the other low throughout the exercise. They move simultaneously or alternately in relation to each other.	D or 2 Gs	Tech, Soc

(2) The first group is high and the second is low and there are constant changes of leadership between them.		D or 2 Gs	Tech, Soc
B. "You're in the country; you're in the city. Show the differences in your body and feelings."		S	Emo, Imag
C. "Life is full of contradictions; let's see what you've got."		S	Emo
D. "Go from one mood to another."	S	S	Emo
E. "Go from one season to another."	S	S	Emo
F. **Extremes**. (Lauren did haughty and friendly; Sally did frantic and calm; Sherry did angular and soft.)		S	Emo, Tech
(1) "Show your transition between two extremes."		S	Art, Emo
(2) "One improviser shows a personal extreme. When an observer gets the idea of what you are doing she will join and do the other extreme. Then you both relate to each other."		S&S	Soc, Emo
G. **Lightness and heaviness**.			
(1) "Experiment with both feelings in different parts of your body."		S	Imag

(2) "Do mirror imaging of lightness and heaviness." Some group ideas we had:	D	D	Imag, Soc
We are as light as daffodils: The group forms petals that eventually blow away.	G	G	Imag
We are sheets billowing in the breeze. (This improv is one that everyone in that class remembered years later.)	D,T,Q	D,T,Q	Imag
H. "One of you be night; one be day. Then, night changes into day."		D	Imag
I. "Go from very loud to very soft (fortissimo to pianissimo)."	S	S	Imag
J. "Go from something in your life that takes a great deal of brute effort to something that has to be done delicately with great care."	S	S	Imag

26 Childhood.

A. "Do a childhood game."	S	S	Imag
B. "Do poses that have the essence of your childhood in them."		S	Imag
C. "What from your childhood do you retain?"		S	Imag, Emo
D. "Recapture something from your childhood that you have lost: a thing or a characteristic or a mood."		S	Imag, Emo

27	**Creatures**.			
	A. "Be creatures who live in the mud, live in the air, move along the earth, move under the earth."	S,G	S,G	Imag
	B. "Any number of you be a creature and move around as one, or as a fantasy creature."	T,Q,G	T,Q,G	Imag, Game
28	**Cartoon**. "Take any number of classmates that you need to make a cartoon of anything that goes on in your life, at work or at home. Then give it a spoken caption." (Dee did two women at a water cooler with one man facing them. The caption was: "Coffee break with the boss breaking it up.")	S&#	S&#	Imag, Game
29	**Choices**. "In life sometimes we have to make a choice, to take one fork in the road rather than the other. But improv is an art form, so we can taste a little bit of **each** fork."		S	Emo
30	**Partner positions**.			
	A. "Stand face to face, side by side, back to back, one behind the other, both facing the same way,	D	D	Art
	one behind the other,	D	D	Art

Theme 3 Structure

Theme 5 Apart and together

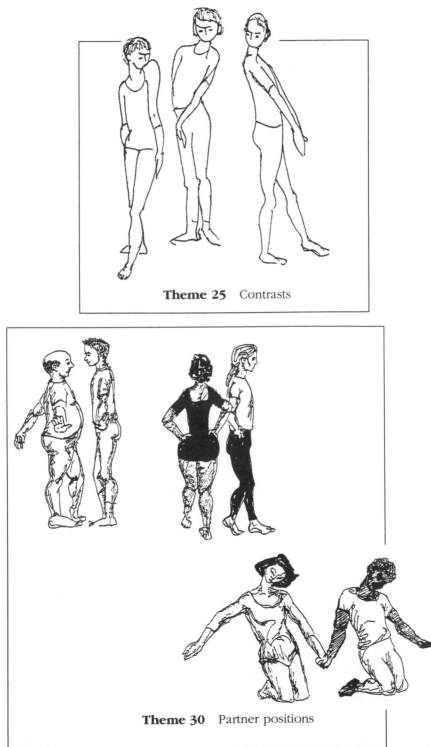

Theme 25 Contrasts

Theme 30 Partner positions

facing different
ways, or
at right angles to each
other."

	Col1	Col2	Col3
B. "Do these positions standing, sitting, or kneeling. "Both partners can be at the same level or at different levels."	D	D	Art
C. "Without talking, partners make smooth transitions together from one position to another, using both relationships and levels."		D	Art
D. "Holding one of each other's hands, partners move out into space, changing positions and levels as they go."		D	Art

31 **Directions**.

	Col1	Col2	Col3
A. "Experiment with moving forward, backward, diagonally, sideways."	S	S	Tech, Art
B. "Consider each of these directions and move in each one of them in a manner that shows what that one means to you."		S	Emo
C. "North, east, south, west—what does each direction mean to you? Do one improv for each."		S	Emo

32 **Elements**.
Everyone in the group
choose one: earth, air,
fire, or water.

A. All earth people move at once, then all air people, etc.	G	G	Imag, Soc
B. Any element can be done as a solo.	S	S	Imag
C. One each of earth, air, fire, and water move together.	Q	Q	Imag, Soc
D. The entire group moves simultaneously. Individuals retain their original choices.	G	G	Imag, Soc, Art

33	Do **Punch and Judy**.	D	D	Imag, Soc
34	**Conflict—climax— outcome.**		S,D,T	Imag, Soc
35	**Disco duo**. "Each moves in the style of some personality from history, literature, current events, etc." (Dina was Lady Macbeth; Gregory was Hamlet.)		D	Imag, Soc, Game
36	**Same people/Different circumstances**. "Two of you 'meet' one way and subsequently relate to each other in a different way or ways."		D	Imag, Soc
37	**Passing on diagonal**. "Start in opposite corners of the room. Exchange corners, passing each other, and continue to pass each other until you both stop."	D	D	Soc
38	**Mirror imaging**. "Do the classic exercise of two people facing each other and moving as if they were each facing a mirror. Initiation of movement passes subtly			

	from one to the other. Effort is for simultaneous exactness of movement."			
	A. Do with duos.	D	D	Soc, Tech, Art
	B. **Mirroring with a difference**. The duo continues to mirror, ignoring the third person. He moves freely around them, between them, or wherever, copying and doing variations on the movements of the duo.	T	T	Soc, Art
39	Define the **canon (fugue)** form ("like singing 'Row, Row, Row Your Boat', except in movement"), and then have the quartet make up its own movement canons.	Q	Q	Art
40	"Open many **doors** or **windows**."	S	S	Imag
41	**Dialogue**.			
	A. "The fingers of one hand dialogue with the fingers of your other hand."	S	S	Imag
	B. "The fingers of one of your hands dialogue with the fingers of someone else's hand."	D	D	Imag, Soc
	C. "Create a dialogue between any two parts of your body."	S	S	Imag
	D. "Dialogue between one part of your body and one part of someone else's body."	D	D	Imag
	E. "Dialogue among three people with one specific body part."	T	T	Imag, Soc

42 **Dreams**.

A. "Move in a dream state, in a daze."	S	S	Imag
B. "Do a real daydream or nightmare that you remember."	S	S	Imag, Emo
C. The whole group moves around as if passing through each other's bodies like phantoms. (We do this every Halloween.)	G	G	Imag
D. "Make a dream come true."	S	S	Imag, Emo

43 **Drumbeat**.

A. Someone creates a phrase on the drum and keeps beating it out while everyone moves.	S&G	S&G	Art, Tech
B. The drumbeat stops but everyone continues to move to that phrase.	S&G	S&G	Art, Tech
C. There is still no drumming; I call out "slower" or "faster" for the tempo of the phrase.	G	G	Tech
D. The drumbeat resumes and all relate freely to others if they choose or continue moving out that same phrase independently. (See **group percussion** heading at the end of this section for further stimuli.)	G	G	Tech, Soc

44 **Emotions**.

A. "Go through the whole gamut of emotions you possess."		S	Emo
B. "Take an emotion that		S	Emo

is uppermost in your life at this moment and invest it in a non-human entity. Improvise that entity. If you're raging, be a 'raging' ocean; calm, a 'calm' lake, etc."

C. "Any one of you start moving in any way you feel. Others who catch on to how you are feeling will join you and use that feeling for their own movement. Be aware of anyone whose feelings change, and respond immediately to that person's feelings with similar feelings of your own."   S&#   Emo, Soc

D. With the entire group on the floor, the teacher calls out the following emotions at brief intervals and anyone who wants to will move: hatred, love, rage, joy, hostility, mourning, anger, loss, delight.   G   G   Emo

45 **Energy**.   S   Tech, Art
Quote from Proust: "My body, which in a long spell of enforced immobility had stored up an accumulation of vital energy, was now obliged, like a spinning top wound and let go, to spend this in every direction."

46	**Exaggeration.**			
	A. "Exaggerate something."		S	Emo, Imag
	B. "One of you set others up in a melodrama. Give it a title."	S&G	S&G	Imag, Art
47	**Dance elements.** Propose these to your class, one word for a session, and see what they do: space, time, energy, motion, color. Also try proposing technical skills like bend, turn, lunge, jump.	G	G	Art
		G	G	Tech
48	**Freedom.** "Make freedom real and meaningful to you personally. Think of someone or something you'd like to be free of, then move to free yourself. You don't have to tell us what you think of."	S	S	Emo
49	**Fabric.** Like any other prop, cloth or ribbon is used first just to see what all its properties are. Then they are used to represent different kinds of real things. Next they evoke emotions. (See "Props", p 82.)	S,D,T,Q,G	S,D,T,Q,G	Imag, Emo, Art, Soc
50	**Friendship.** Just say the word and ask if any duo or trio in the class would like to use it. Natural groupings will likely occur. Also one person may take the	D,T&#	D,T&#	Emo, Soc

Theme 34 Conflict—climax—outcome

Theme 38 Mirroring

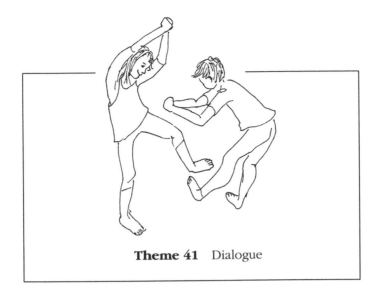

Theme 41 Dialogue

Theme 44 Emotions

initiative in approaching another or others.

51 The **floor**.

A. "Use the floor as anything beneath you."	S	S	Imag
B. "This is not the floor; it is the earth."	S	S	Imag
C. "Use the floor as a surface (ice, mud),	S	S	Imag
springboard,	S	S	Imag, Tech
level to go below."	S	S	Imag

52 **Floor pattern**.

"One of you go to each corner. Imagine a floor pattern (a path visualized by you as being drawn on the floor) that returns you to your corner."

A. "One at a time, trace that path, going out from your corner, following it, then returning to your corner."	S	S	Art
B. "Now, all four of you follow your floor patterns at the same time, not interfering with or relating to the others, and returning to your corners."	Q	Q	Art
C. "When two or more of you meet, freeze, then go on; relate any way you wish; do motions of hello, or act as if you are saying hello, but are in a hurry."	D,T,Q	D,T,Q	Art, Soc

53 **Fear**.

A. "Move out any big fear of yours."	S	S	Emo

B. I quote from Nietzsche: " 'Whoever fights monsters should see to it that in the process he does not become a monster. And when you look long into an abyss, the abyss also looks into you.' React to something you fear. Then be the thing you fear."		S	Emo, Art
C. "I saw a child on a crowded bus clinging to his mother's skirt with one hand and clutching a rubber 'Superman' doll in the other. When you're afraid, what is it you hold onto?"		S	Emo
D. "Work with a fear you have overcome."		S	Emo

54 **Fight**.

A. "Have a snowball fight."	S,D,T,Q,G	S,D,T,Q,G	Tech
B. "Punch and kick each other without touching."	D	D	Tech, Emo
C. "Start out with an angry encounter toward your partner. See what develops."		D	Tech, Emo, Soc
D. "Do '**attitudes of combat**' without touching."	D	D	Tech

55 "Face the palms of your hands to the **palms** of your partner's hands without touching. Go on from there until you both stop."	D	D	Tech

Theme 47   Dance elements: exploring technical movement

Theme 51   The floor

Theme 53 Fear

Theme 55 "Face palms of your hands to palms of partner's hands."

56	**Hails and farewells**.		
	A. "Say goodbye to something or someone and say hello to something or someone else."	S S	Imag
	B. "Say hello and goodbye to someone you dislike, someone you like, or someone you haven't seen in a long time."	S S	Imag, Emo
	C. "Do an **opening number** for a musical show, both greeting the audience and giving them a hint of what's to come."	S,D,T,Q,G S,D,T,Q,G	Imag, Art
	D. "Move around, greeting each other person in the room." We call this improv **Reunion** and use it after summer and vacation breaks. (See themes 150-155.)	G G	Soc
57	**Gifts**.		
	A. "Gather things— flowers, branches, clouds, stars—and give them to each other."	G G	Soc, Emo
	B. "If there's someone in class you dislike for no reason but want to get along with, do a solo in which you give that person beautiful things."	S S	Emo
	C. "Give yourself something you've always wanted."	S S	Emo

D. The birthday person sits in the middle of the floor and each classmate gathers or fashions some gift. (They have given apparel, jewelry, massage, flowers, food, hugs.)	S&G	S&G	Emo, Soc

58 **Guilt**.
Sara said she took a lot of guilt upon herself. I gave her this theme: "Take the guilt of the whole world upon yourself since its very beginning."

		S	Emo

59 **Hugs**.

A. "Hug yourself, experiencing any feelings it brings."	S	S	Emo
B. "Hug a childhood or current possession (doll, teddy bear, etc.)."	S	S	Emo
C. "Recall from the past anyone you'd like to hug again, or never did and want to now."	S	S	Emo
D. "Do a memorable hug you've had or given."	S	S	Emo
E. "Think of all the people you'd like to give hugs to in the future, and give them now."	S	S	Emo
F. "Take partners and give each other one hug, for real. Now, continue a series of hugs without touching." (This is an excellent introduction to	D	D	Art

stylizing: an outline gesture that conveys full intent. I always cite the snake that can be represented by a little wavy line.)

G. "Could anyone here use a group hug?" (Being the focus of an entire group's hug is very healing. If you know a student has had a recent operation, bereavement, family loss, etc., do offer this to her or him.)	S&G	S&G	Emo, Soc
60 **Open group.** "Would anyone like to direct the group in some theme or movement you have in mind?"	S&G	S&G	Art
61 **Orchestra.**			
A. "Play an instrument you've dreamed of playing."	S	S	Imag
B. "Be a musical instrument."	S	S	Imag
C. "Take turns conducting an entire orchestra of your actual classmates; or choose a duo, trio, quartet, or quintet composed of them."	S&#	S&#	Imag, Art
62 Theme: "One thing touches another and changes all relationships around them." (I saw Belgian sculptor Pol Bury's kinetic sculpture at the Guggenheim Museum in New York City. Any little part that		G	Imag, Soc

moved would make the other parts rearrange.)

63	**Freeze/Stretch.** "All move freely but freeze on drumbeat. On cymbal, extend movement toward one or two others until you touch. Then break and continue freely until the next drumbeat."	G	G	Tech, Soc
64	**Dependent.** "The safety of all is dependent on one."	S&G	S&G	Imag, Soc
65	Do the group and a bully, a stranger, or a helpless or injured person.	G	G	Imag, Soc
66	**Crocus.** "Several be crocuses coming up through the earth: The rest of the group be the earth."	G	G	Imag, Soc
67	**Seed.** "In one incident, find the seed of another."		S	Imag, Emo
68	**Hands.** "Let's explore the hand."			
	A. "Look at your own hand and see what its parts do technically."	S	S	Imag, Tech
	B. "Use the hand in relation to yourself, others, things."	S	S	Imag, Tech
	C. "Use the hand for signals we all understand in this society."	S	S	Tech
	D. We ask a student to stand behind a screen with only a hand showing. We call out	S	S	Tech

various ways for it to be used: gentle, murderous, resistant, threatening, helpful.

E. "The focus is on your own hands."	S	S	Imag, Tech
F. "Everyone suggest ideas for using hands with the entire group." (This is an excellent group unifier; everyone gets absorbed and feels related.)	G	G	Imag, Soc, Emo

69 **Increments**.

"Every day after the winter equinox one sees the daylight lengthening bit by bit. Let's take this gradual increase as our theme."

A. "Do one movement. Do it again and add another movement. Do those two and then add a third. Continue adding movements."		S	Tech, Art
B. "Quantity into quality: Do one movement or movement phrase over and over again." (This is a good time to discuss the characteristics of monotony; the "whirling" dervishes [an ascetic Muslim sect that worships through ecstatic dancing]; the general uses of repetitive movement; or the deleterious effects of repetitive movements as we work at machines.)	S,D,T,Q,G	S,D,T,Q,G	Tech, Art

C. "Add to a one-to-one relationship: Each time you meet your partner, add something to make the relationship grow or deteriorate."	D	D	Emo
D. Ask the question to the group: "Can you think of a theme that starts with one person, then requires two, then three, etc.?"	G	G	Imag, Emo
E. "An eruption doesn't happen suddenly; it builds. Annoyance becomes rage, dislike can become hate, delight can become ecstasy. Take something that builds like that." (Bren and Dee did chums becoming more and more playful. Selma and Cher did fetuses growing and discovering their own and each other's parts; they were both pregnant women. May and Greg did repression that ended in tragedy.)	S,D	S,D	Imag, Emo

70 **Hoops**.

A. "Take one hoop, two hoops, three hoops, and do anything with them."	S	S	Tech
B. "It is a hoop of flames."	S	S	Imag
C. I place three hoops on the floor, several feet apart from each other, and say:	S	S	Imag

(1) "As you go across the floor, do a hop, a jump, or something active inside each hoop."	S	S	Tech
(2) "Show three different sides of yourself, or three stages of your life, or a progression of three of anything."		S	Imag, Emo
(3) "Follow the leader: One of you lead the group; they will copy whatever you do inside each hoop."	S	S	Imag, Soc, Tech
D. "No hoops now; move around as if you had a hoop."	S	S	Imag
E. "All stand in a circle and pass one hoop around."	G	G	Imag, Soc
F. "Two of you share one hoop."	D	D	Soc
G. "Two of you relate to each other, each with your own hoop."	D	D	Soc, Imag
H. "Three of you have two hoops to work with."	T	T	Imag, Soc
I. "Inside this hoop there is a deep nothing." (A number of students have, at different times, used this theme to get to deep, personal stuff.)		S	Imag, Emo
71 **The knot**. The "knot" is made by one person lying on the floor in as contorted a position as possible. The	S&S	S&S	Soc

person who opens the "knot" must do it carefully (this improv takes a lot of time); if at any moment the "knot" doesn't feel gently handled, it will contract again. We all watch until the "knot" is completely opened and lying utterly relaxed. Throughout the semester, students ask for this improv whenever they feel particularly under stress.

72	**Kaleidoscope**.	T, Q	T, Q	Soc, Art

Ann takes a pose. Bill fits in and around her. Then Carlos fits in and around them both. Ann then runs to another position. Bill follows, and Carlos follows Bill. Ann always holds her position until Carlos has fit in and around Bill. **Kaleidoscope** is done very quickly; Ann runs to a new pose just as soon as Carlos has taken his pose. (Several trios or quartets doing this simultaneously in a large space has choreographic effect. See theme 158 for further variations of **kaleidoscope**.)

73	**Laughter**.	S	S	Emo

"Do all kinds of laughter: bright, bitter, tearful. Do not use any sound."

74 **Levels**.
Lying, sitting, kneeling, crouching, standing, "elevation" (off the floor).

A. "Take one movement and repeat it on each different level."		S	Tech
B. "Move within one level only."	S	S	Tech
C. "Move within two levels of your choice."	S	S	Tech
D. "Move around in space, using all the levels."		S	Tech
E. Ann moves on one level, Bud on another. Whenever Ann changes her level, Bud changes his.	D	D	Tech, Soc
F. Three-level sequence: lying, kneeling, standing. Ann lies, Bob kneels, Cal stands. Ann goes to kneel, Bob to stand, Cal to lie. Ann goes to stand, Bob to lie, Cal to kneel. This sequence continues. The responses to Ann's change to her next level are immediate. This is only for a skilled trio.		T	Tech, Soc

75 **Limitations**.

A "limitation" means, for us, imposing one physical restraint while leaving the rest of the body free, or putting one precondition upon any number of persons, leaving them otherwise free. The limitation can be suggested by the teacher or by the participants themselves. It is among the best stimuli I know of for eliciting un-

usual, subtle, and un-
planned movements.

A. "Clasp your hands. Otherwise you can move anywhere and any way you wish."	S	S	Tech
B. "Arrange both arms in a fixed position; move freely otherwise."	S	S	Tech
C. "Hold any part of your body with one hand. Keep this limitation while you move freely otherwise."	S	S	Tech
D. "Touch each other's right elbows. Keep that contact no matter what else you do."	D	D	Tech, Soc
E. "Make any joining between you, and keep it while you move freely. (They might link right arms.)"	D	D	Tech, Soc
F. "Stand shoulder to shoulder. Now move freely otherwise."	T	T	Tech, Soc
G. "Each of you place one hand on the body of another trio member. Now move freely otherwise."	T	T	Tech, Soc
H. "Place your right foot on the floor where it can touch at least one other person's foot. Aside from this limitation, you are all free to move any way you can.	Q&#	Q&#	Tech, Soc
I. "Hold hands and keep moving until you all stop."	G	G	Tech, Soc
J. "Each of you place one hand on a wall, a barre, or the floor.	G	G	Tech, Soc

Theme 66 Crocus

Theme 70 Hoops

Theme 71 The knot

Theme 74 Levels

Keep it there but re-
late to others as you
move."

76	**Melt**.	S	S	Imag

"You are an icicle or a
candle. Melt all the way
down." (This is the most
acceptable theme for the
utter beginner.)

77 **Message sending**.

A. The group stands in a circle or on the diagonal. Ann starts a movement toward Bill. Bill takes the same movement and sends it on to Carlos. Then Carlos sends it to Dianne, etc. All hold the move as a pose until it's time to move again.	Q&#	Q&#	Soc, Imag
B. **Gossip**. Ann starts a movement. Bill does something with her movement. Carlos does something with Bill's movement. This process continues.	Q&#	Q&#	Soc, Imag
C. A ball, hoop, or baton can follow the same principle: It can be passed on the same way it is received.	Q&#	Q&#	Imag, Soc
D. Each one in the circle can receive, handle, and pass on the object in his or her own personal variation.	Q&#	Q&#	Imag, Soc

78 **Minimize, maximize**.

A. "Take a small movement and magnify it."	S	S	Imag, Tech, Art

B. "Take a big movement and minimize it."	S	S	Imag, Tech, Art
C. "Take a concern in your life. Do it in little movements or do it in big movements (underplay or overplay)."		S	Emo
D. "Take a movement you do every day and minimize or maximize it." (Sara did picking up the telephone receiver. Ben did a combination of little and extravagant hellos.)	S	S	Imag, Art

79 Magnet.

A. "One partner is a magnet, the other is irresistibly drawn all around the room."	D	D	Imag, Tech
B. "Start with two magnetizing each other; gradually every one in the group joins, one at a time or whenever you wish, until all in group are 'magnetic' in duos, trios, or whatever you fall into."	D,T,G	D,T,G	Imag, Soc
C. Two who are equally magnetic spar for control.		D	Tech

80 Masks.

A. At Halloween I offer actual masks that only cover the eyes, varied in color and design to suit different needs. A solo may use one in the front worn simultaneously with one in	S,D	S,D	Imag, Art, Emo

the back of the head
or may use one at a
time and alternate be-
tween the two. Solos
or duos take as many
masks as they wish
and do improvs sepa-
rately or together.

B. Each person in the group fashions an imaginary mask and wears it for a solo or with another or others.	S,D&#	S,D&#	Imag, Art, Emo

81 New.
One year I said to the
class, "I just had my studio painted, and when I
walked in after it was
dry, it seemed like a
fresh, new beginning—
causing me to feel nostalgic, saddened, and
stimulated all at the same
time. So, for improv to-
night, do: 'Beginning
anew, beginning
afresh.' "

	S	S	Emo

82 Nature.

A. "Battle with the el-ements."	S	S	Imag
B. "Be an earthworm aer-ating the earth."	S	S	Imag
C. "I had a confrontation with nature today. I was sitting at my table, which faces west, just at sundown. Suddenly my whole face glowed, bathed by the sunlight. I thought of how the sun came from afar to light my immediate		S	Imag, Emo, Art

surroundings. So, our theme: Your most genuine moment of personal consciousness of nature."

D. "Do an outdoor landscape so vividly that we can see it."	S	S	Imag
E. "Be in your environment with another (imaginary) person."		S	Imag, Emo
F. "Now take just one aspect of that landscape that you feel is its essence, and either be that essence or be how it makes you feel."		S	Imag, Emo, Art

83 **Add-a-Person: Make something new by adding you**.	S&#	S&#	Imag, Art

Two people hold hands and get into any position they can hold. A third person enters, taking hand, arms, or in any way moving the other two into a position for three. Then a fourth comes and changes the position of the three to make it a design for four. This process continues. (This is excellent for making a shy student assertive enough to be "included," and for getting a static situation moving again.)

84 **One-Word themes**.			

There are two uses for single-word themes:

A. When a student stands in front of me	S,D	S,D	Tech, Emo

in anticipation of my selecting a word particularly suited to him or her, I choose a word that will solidify the student's present style, give the student a taste of another style, or help overcome some personal technical or emotional quirk.

B. With a skilled group of students, I take the risk of having one stand before them and have the classmates call out to the improviser any word they think relevant. Teasing and light hostilities may be shown in the selection of the words, but in a strong, solid, and confident group, all goes well. Good single words: cloud, hiding, fearful, pulse, push-and-pull, jelly, arrow, explosion, angles, combat.

B.	S,D	S,D	Tech, Emo

85 **Opposites**.
A. "Do one strong feeling of yours and then its opposite, so you can see what comes out."

B. "Do some extremes in you."

C. "Move from one extreme to another—of anything, technical or emotional."

A.		S	Emo
B.	S	S	Emo
C.		S	Emo, Tech

D. "Do a resolution of ex-tremes."		S	Emo, Art
86 ***Nuances***. "Set two distinctly differ-ent positions. Then start with the first position and change it very gradually. See what nuances it passes through to get to the second position."		S	Tech, Art
87 **Potion**. "Brew up a potion, all of you, and then use that brew in any way you need it—for yourself and with others."	G	G	Imag
88 **Parallels**. Explain that parallels do not have to be only straight lines; that curves of the body can be parallel.			
A. "Make all the different parallels of parts of your own body that you can devise."	S	S	Tech
B. "Make parallels of parts of your body with the floor or the wall."	S	S	Tech
C. "Two or more do par-allels with each other."	D,T,Q,G	D,T,Q,G	Tech
D. "A duo, in positions parallel to each other, move across the floor, changing tempo or step but not po-sition."	D	D	Tech
89 **Power**. "Do something you're go-ing to make happen."		S	Emo

90 **Poems**.
We have done improvs to:

A. Poetry written by classmates.	S,D,T,Q,G	S,D,T,Q,G	Art, Emo
B. Famous poetry that moves us.	S,D,T,Q,G	S,D,T,Q,G	Art, Emo
C. Quotes brought in by me and class members.	S,D,T,Q,G	S,D,T,Q,G	Art, Emo
D. Poetry spoken sponta-neously by the group: Each one speaks a line while improvis-ing, picking up on and extending the thought of the preced-ing improviser. The line may be created verbally before, dur-ing, or after the improv.	G	G	Art, Soc, Emo

91 **Percussion as both in-strument and prop**.

A. Each takes a different percussion instru-ment and takes turns doing improvs with them.	S	S	Tech, Art
B. One student plays a phrase on any, sev-eral, or all of the per-cussion while the group moves.	S&G	S&G	Art
C. The group breaks up into duos, trios, fours, etc., and everyone moves simultane-ously, playing the in-struments in their own little groups.	D,T,Q	D,T,G	Art
D. I lay out drums, cym-bals, bells of various kinds, tambourines, tri-	S	S	Emo

angles, maracas, etc.,
and suggest that any-
one can use any of
them for emotional
content.

92 **Poses/Statues**.

A. For duo: "Move to-gether until you create a pose you want to hold. Move again and hold. Move again and hold. Go until you stop." (This is also good for trios and fours.)	D,T,Q	D,T,Q	Tech, Art
B. Each pose leads to an-other, to tell a story or an emotion.	S	S	Art, Emo
C. "Greg, mold Nan into a statue. Then you and Pat can take posi-tions in relation to that statue that will have a meaning when seen as a whole."	T	T	Art
D. The entire group be-comes a statue.	G	G	Art

93 **Picture postcards**.
Good for holidays, the
end of a semester, birth-
days, good-byes, returns
after vacations or ill-
nesses, and so on.

A. "One student, use as many of your class-mates as you wish to form a picture greet-ing card." All remain motionless, facing the one for whom the "card" is meant. When the recipient ap-plauds or says thank	S&#	S&#	Art

Theme 75 Limitations

Theme 83 Add-a-Person

Theme 92 Poses/Statues

you, the "card" becomes animated.				
B. The group arranges itself into an old-fashioned family portrait. When the cameraperson "clicks," posers shift into another position or change facial expressions.	S&G	S&G		Art
C. The entire group arranges itself into a pose appropriate to the holiday being celebrated.	G	G		Art

94 Qualities.

A. "Move to the quality of a song—its feeling, not what it specifically says."	S	S		Emo, Art
B. "Move as if you were made of glass (fragile, transparent), metal, wood, or cloth."	S	S		Tech, Art

95 Rhythm.   S   S   Art

"Take a rhythm of your daily life. In the course of your day there are many rhythms: You arise slowly or abruptly. You may eat breakfast slowly or bolt it down. You may run for the bus or subway. You may work sitting down, moving around, or to the rhythm of a machine. You may be conscious of some rhythm going on outside your window, in the street, or in the neighboring apartment, house, or area."

96 **Resistance**.

A. "Do someone or something you are re-sisting."	S	S	Emo
B. For duo: "Resist each other, touching or not touching."	D	D	Emo
C. Two groups are pitted against each other.	2 Gs	2 Gs	Emo, Art
D. "Resist the natural ele-ments—a storm, a strong wind or gale, excessive heat, or a torrential downpour of rain."	S,D,T,Q,G	S,D,T,Q,G	Emo, Art, Imag

97 **Rope**.

A. "What can you do with a rope?"	S	S	Tech, Imag
B. Rope pulling: Every-one, in his own per-sonal space, experiments with dif-ferent kinds of ropes—different ways of pulling them in every direction and different uses for them.	G	G	Tech, Imag
C. Tug-of-war: Set up the group into sides using an imaginary rope.	G	G	Tech, Imag, Soc
D. Now do the tug-of-war in slow motion.	G	G	Tech, Imag, Soc, Art

98 **Rituals**.

"You come from another place. Teach the class the movements you do in 'your country.' Describe verbally what movements your country uses for what they believe in." (My students have done believers in only straight-line movements, sun		G	Imag, Art, Soc

worshipers using special arm movements, deity worshipers using different kinds of bows, arrows, and spears.)

Then the group does rituals in that style in relation to the following: birth, death, marriage, war, victory, magic, religion, harvest, hunting, healing, adolescence, courtship, fertility, work, gathering crops, masks, sowing and reaping, exorcising evil spirits, strength for battle, dreaming about animal clan, rainmaking, hailing a new chief, and incantations for rain, sun, crops protection, forgiveness.	S,D,T,Q,G	S,D,T,Q,G	Imag, Tech, Art

99   Snow.

A. "Build a snowperson."	S,D,T,Q,G	S,D,T,Q,G	Imag, Art
B. "Have a snowball fight."	D,T,Q,G	D,T,Q,G	Imag, Tech
C. "Take a sled ride."	S,D,T	S,D,T	Imag, Tech
D. "Ride on a toboggan."	T,Q,G	T,Q,G	Imag, Tech
E. "Walk in the snow."	S	S	Imag
F. "Be a snowflake."	S,D,T,Q,G	S,D,T,Q,G	Imag

100   The sun.

A. "Grow toward a source of light."	S,G	S,G	Imag, Soc
B. "Be a source of life."	S	S	Imag, Emo
C. "Set up planetary tracks around the sun."	G	G	Art
D. "Be the sun."	S	S	Imag
E. "Create a drought."	G	G	Imag

101   Silence.

"In speech we have pauses and silences. In movement there are very meaningful moments of	S	S	Imag, Emo, Art

complete immobility. Do
some subject material
that requires you to stop,
motionless, for genuine
reasons connected with
your theme."

102 **Setbacks**.		S	Imag, Emo, Art

"Just when spring was
definitely (or at least we
thought so) here, we had
a blizzard and it looked
and felt like winter again.
Let's take as theme: **set-
backs**—something we ex-
pect to continue in a
certain way that takes another turn or reverses
itself."

103 **Stretching**.

"We know that stretching
must come after warm-
ups, but improv time
comes after a lot of class
movement."

A. "Stretch your body as if it were made of many elastics."	S	S	Tech
B. "Stand or lie and let two 'stretchers' help you pull your legs and arms gently beyond what you could do by yourself."	S&#	S&#	Tech, Soc

(Throughout any
stretching, I always
keep up a stream of
talk, reminding every-
one to give tender
and loving care to this
unique body they are
working on, to ap-
preciate the class-
mate's individuality
of structure, to be

attentive to the stret-
chee's needs.)

C. "Anyone need a group stretch?" This means that the stretchee can lie down, with closed eyes, and have the rest of the group stretch arms, legs, and torso, and loosen head and neck. I tell the stretchee to say "thank you" when completely relaxed, but I generally have to say it for them, as they want the stretching never to end.	S&G	S&G	Tech, Soc
D. "Pretend you have an elastic between your hands,	S	S	Tech
between your ankles,	S	S	Tech
between any two places on your body you want,	S	S	Tech
tied between a partner's ankle and your hand, or	D	D	Tech, Soc
held by your partner's hands and yours (one elastic between you)."	D	D	Tech, Soc

104 **The stage**.

These are themes related to the position of the performer on the stage.

A. "Use upstage (the part of the stage furthest from the audience) for a mysterious mood."	S	S	Art
B. "Use the side stages for themes removed from the main action, half-hidden from the audience."	S	S	Art

C. "Use the center stage to be in the full spotlight."	S	S	Art
D. "Use downstage (the front of a stage) for the most personal encounter between audience and performer."	S	S	Art

105 Senses.

A. "You are a camera eye."	S	S	Imag, Art
B. "Close your eyes and put your hands forward at shoulder level. When you touch someone else in the group, move together."	G	G	Soc
C. "Move around employing all your senses: touch, taste, smell, hearing, sight. If any of these sensory stimuli recall something or someone you associate with that sense, move that out."	S	S	Imag, Emo

106 Symmetry/Asymmetry.

A. "Experiment with symmetrical poses with your own body, in place, or	S	S	Art
with a partner." (Note: This is one of the rare occasions for improvisers to see themselves in a mirror.)	D	D	Art
B. "In place, do movements the same on both sides of your body, or	S	S	Art, Tech
with a partner standing or sitting	D	D	Art, Tech, Soc

alongside, your out-
side arms maintaining
the symmetry."

C. "Stage a symmetrical pose for the entire group."	S&G	S&G	Art
D. "Create symmetrical movement for the entire group."	S&G	S&G	Art
E. "Start with a symmetrical stance, pattern, or movement phrase and change one thing to make it asymmetrical."	S,D,T,Q,G	S,D,T,Q,G	Art

107 Shadows.

A. "Make shadows on the floor or on the wall."	S	S	Imag
B. "Play with your shadow or your reflection in (an imaginary) mirror."	S	S	Imag
C. "How do you feel about seeing shadows in your house or on the street?"	S	S	Emo
D. "One person move behind the other as if you were her shadow."	D	D	Soc
E. "In front of a wall, create a shadow and leave it as an imprint of yourself, or	S	S	Imag, Emo
move around, watching the shadows you cast." (This is most fun on a wall that actually does catch shadows.)	S,D,T,Q,G	S,D,T,Q,G	Imag, Soc

108 Sound.

A. "Move around until some sound comes out of you. The group out front will echo		S&G	Art, Soc

your sound immedi-
ately as a chorus. Con-
tinue to move, make a
sound, and wait for
the echo, repeating
this until you want to
stop."

B. "Make your own sounds that go with the movements you are doing."		S	Art, Imag, Emo
C. "Choose any kind of bell and voice that sound while you move to it."		S	Art, Imag
D. "All in the group move and sound your bells together." (Some feel a little silly, but it's lots of fun.)	G	G	Art, Imag, Soc

109 **Sand**.

A. "Experiment with sand as a sensory ex- perience."	S	S	Imag
B. "Build something, with a partner or with others, on the beach."	S&#	S&#	Imag, Soc, Art
C. "Play with others on the beach (catch ball, make pyramid, etc.)."	G	G	Imag, Soc
D. "You are caught in a sandstorm."	S,D,T,Q,G	S,D,T,Q,G	Imag
E. "You are on a desert of sand with no water."	S,D,T,Q,G	S,D,T,Q,G	Imag
F. "On a beach, contrast moving on dry sand and on wet sand."	S	S	Imag
G. "Do Native American sandpainting, which is created of colored sands, used to help heal a tribe member, and then destroyed."		S	Imag

Theme 96   Resistance

Theme 97   Rope

Theme 106   Symmetry/Asymmetry

110 **Talk**.	G	Soc

Although I discourage talk in our nonverbal setting, there was one session where the students came in all bubbling to communicate with each other. I suggested that they actually converse, as a group, while they were moving through the warm-ups, and then that we all watch everyone move while talking reflectively about whatever thoughts were currently in mind. It turned out to be a memorable class.

111 **Tightrope**.	S,D	S,D	Imag, Art, Soc, Tech

This is one of the great classics—good for the novice through most experienced. Whether for solo or duo, I heighten the tension by calling out, "No net!"

112 **Space**.

This is one of those mighty words that the teacher throws out to the group for their suggestions as to themes. Here are some of theirs and some of mine:

A. "How do you feel about being in a spacious place?"		S	Emo
B. "Think of space around you as having a shape."	S	S	Imag
C. "Carve out a place for yourself in the air."		S	Imag

D. "Make this space your own."		S	Imag, Emo
E. "It's low overhead but there is lots of space around."	S	S	Imag, Emo
F. "There is lots of space above but none around."	S	S	Imag, Emo
G. Space between people: "One person take the group and arrange them with space in between—equal spaces between individuals, or a space between a solo and a duo, or two together and three others apart, etc."		S&G	Imag, Art, Soc
H. "Make space for others on a seat, at the table, in a cramped bus."	S	S	Soc
I. "You are 'spaced out.'"		S	Emo
J. "You are in outer space."	S,D,T,Q,G	S,D,T,Q,G	Imag
K. "You are in a close, intimate space, a narrow space, or far or unlimited space."	S	S	Imag, Emo
L. "Alternate squeezing into and expanding in space."	S	S	Imag, Emo
M. "How do you feel about sharing space, invasion of your private space, or cluttered versus bare space?"		S	Emo
N. "Think of all the spaces you inhabit during your day and how you feel in them,		S	Emo

physically and emotionally."

113 **Living it over**.	S	Emo

"Take a theme, incident, or relationship and play it two different ways."

114 **The unexpected**.	S	Emo

"I have been treating my African violets democratically though they're supposed to have special treatment. Today, to my surprise, they bloomed. The theme is something unexpected—good or otherwise."

115 **Tempos**.
(I always make clear the difference between rhythm and tempo: "The waltz in 3/4 time is always a waltz no matter whether the tempo is fast or slow.")

A. "To bring the range of tempos to mind, let's say some adjectives that are suggestive." (We get: slow, fast, quick, sprightly, moderate, jittery, calm, nervous, rapid, lethargic.) "Now, think of the tempos with which you do things throughout your day."	S	Imag
B. "Go from lying to standing, varying tempos for ascent and descent as you repeat this continual changing of levels."	S	Tech
C. "One partner start from a lying position and one from a stand-	D	Tech, Soc

ing, and change levels and tempos as you will."

D. A solo inside a group circle varies tempos of movement, and the group responds immediately.   S&G   Tech, Soc

E. **Accelerate/ Decelerate**.

(1) Each individual takes a movement and accelerates it, then moves it into space. Then all accelerate movement together. (One group did shelter from rain.)   S&#   S&#   Tech, Soc

(2) "Accelerate an emotion." (One group did a frightening phone call.)   S   Tech, Emo

(3) "Decelerate an emotion." (One group went from hysterical laughter to depression.)   S   Tech, Emo

116 **Two groups**.

"What can two groups do together?" Examples of some groups' ideas follow.

A. Someone from one group does something with someone from another group.   S&G   S&G   Soc

B. The group forms two circles. Each circle tries to prevent the person in the center of their circle from joining the person in the center of the other circle without touching. (This is an   G   G   Soc excellent tension-breaking exercise for a class or workshop where beginners and experienced are together.)

C. Two groups in irregular clumps stand facing each other. They rise high on their toes or descend into a crouch in opposition to each other. This continues, each adjusting their tempo to the others in their own group and to the opposite group. (This has always been done with enormously silent and concentrated absorption.)	2 Gs	2 Gs	Tech, Soc

117 **Metamorphoses**.

A. "Show three different related things and the transition from one to the other."	S	S	Imag, Art
B. "Show something going from small to larger to largest." (One group did: drop of water, shower, ocean.)	S	S	Imag
C. "Show three different stages of an emotion." (One group did: giggle, laughter, hilarity.)		S	Imag, Emo
D. Laura gave the group this theme: "Show any three stages of color, like a leaf that goes from green to yellow to sere."		S	Imag

E. I devised this for an   S   Art, Emo
   actor as nourishment
   from his former glory
   days: "Tree into
   acorn."

118 **Whole**.   S   S   Imag
   "Spring rain, spring sun,
   spring earth, spring flow-
   ers, spring breezes—
   these are all part of a
   whole, and together produce spring. Think of
   component parts that
   make a whole." (Greg
   did five senses, Ron did
   New York after dark.)

119 **Words**.   S   Imag, Art
   "Accompany yourself
   with your own words.
   The words can be uttered
   before, after, or during
   the movement. The
   words can be repeated,
   cut into syllables,
   stretched out, etc. The
   'words' themselves can
   be nonsense words."

120 **Woman**.
   A. "The theme is   S   S   Art, Emo
      woman." (Examples
      from one of my
      classes: Alma rose
      from sleep beside her
      husband, put on lip-
      stick quickly, and lay
      down again. Audrey
      stood on a pedestal as
      statue, jumped down
      and washed the base
      of the pedestal, then
      got back on the pedes-
      tal again.)

B. "Do something you weren't permitted to do as a little girl because you weren't a boy." (Tina did boccie ball.)	S	S	Imag, Emo
C. "Be the little girl you were and/or the little girl you'd like to be."		S	Imag, Emo
D. "Be the woman you are; then the woman you would like to be."		S	Imag, Emo
E. "Go from girl to woman."		S	Imag, Emo, Art

121 Walk/Run.
(Be sure feet are well warmed up before this.)

A. "Start yourself off on a walk. Don't think; just let your body go." We call this "The Walk."	S	S	Imag
B. "The entire group walks around. At any time, anyone can call out a 'way' to walk and others immediately respond." For instance: tired, happy, bouncy, angry, sad.	G	G	Soc
C. "Walk side by side. One of you may change the rhythm, tempo, or direction of the walk while the other(s) respond(s) immediately to keep in step."	D,T	D,T	Tech, Soc
D. Do the same but on a light, steady run.	D	D	Tech, Soc
E. "The entire group walks freely around	G	G	Tech, Soc

the room, separately.
Gradually you will
move together so that
all of you are walking
side by side, shoulder
to shoulder." (This is
excellent as a unifier
after a class or work-
shop break.)

F. "Experiment with your own running: tempos, energy, directions, floor patterns, etc." (This can be done solo while others watch the experimentation, or the entire group can do it.)	S, G	S, G	Tech
G. "Combine running and walking in sequences you can repeat, with three different directions." (For instance: run forward, walk backward, run in a circle.)		S	Tech
H. "Think of reasons that would force you to run."	S	S	Imag

122 **Water**.

A. "Be any form of water."	S	S	Imag
B. "Move as if underwater."	S	S	Imag
C. "Walk through water that is up to your waist."	S	S	Imag
D. "Be one wave."	S	S	Imag
E. "Be several waves."	D&#	D&#	Imag
F. "Be an ocean."	G	G	Imag
G. "One run along the edge of the ocean."	S&G	S&G	Imag

H. "One dive in and out of the ocean."	S&G	S&G	Imag
I. "Do an experience you've had with water."	S	S	Imag, Emo

123 **Weather**.
The actual weather at the time of a class or workshop is an ever-present source of themes. Cold, hot, rain, snow, thunder, lightning, clouds, wind, hail, icy, frosty, overcast—all provide the basis for the themes:

A. "How does (the phenomenon) make you feel? Don't tell us; do it."	S	S	Tech, Emo
B. "Be (the phenomenon)."	S	S	Tech, Emo

The following themes are all related to **yourself**.

124 A. **Autobiography**. "When I was a kid . . . "		S	Imag, Emo
B. "Do the movements of a relative or friend."	S	S	Imag
C. "See yourself historically—as a person with antecedents, as one in a long chain of evolution."		S	Imag, Art
D. **Heritage**. "Be a grandparent, then your parent, then yourself."		S	Imag, Art, Emo
125 "Take something from your summer and something from this autumn and put them together for this coming winter."		S	Imag, Art

126	"Instead of doing things in your usual pattern, you break (or broke) away."	S	Imag. Emo
127	I quote from Collete: " 'Look for a long time at what pleases you, and longer still at what pains you.' Move to this."	S	Emo, Art
128	"Think of some way that violence was committed against you. Then deal with it."	S	Emo
129	"Go into something so deeply that you 'come out the other side.' "	S	Emo, Art
130	"Do 'Everything in the world is mine.' " (I give this to someone who is modest, shy, withdrawn.)	S	S	Emo, Imag
131	**Central theme**.		
	A. "Move out a central theme in your life."	S	Imag, Art
	B. "Go away from your central theme, but return to it."	S	Imag, Art, Emo
	C. "Teach this central theme to the others in the group."	S&G	Art, Soc
	D. "Watch the group do your central theme; then they watch your solo in whatever way you react."	G&S	Art, Soc, Emo
132	**Your day**. "Do a typical, or specifically remembered, day of yours."	S	Imag
133	**Introductions**.		
	A. "Introduce yourself without talking."	S	Imag

B. "Spell your name out in movement."	S	S	Imag, Art
C. "Relate first to one person or thing, then to another person or thing—do as many as you wish, to bring out all your facets."		S	Imag, Emo, Art

134 **Facets**.

A. "Do all the facets of the kind of person you are."		S	Imag, Emo

135 **Self-Shaping**.

A. "Distribute all the different parts of you to the elements, then bring them back together."		S	Imag, Emo, Art
B. "Add something to yourself that you've always wanted— something physical, emotional, etc."		S	Imag, Emo, Art
C. "Put your ideal self together as you'd like to be physically, emotionally, and in any other way."		S	Imag, Emo, Art

Special Themes

The themes that follow are special ones and don't follow the pattern of the themes I've just described. The themes have been left uncategorized, apply to both beginners and experienced students, are useful for any number of participants, and may lead to artistic, emotional, imaginative, societal, or technical responses. The number in the left margin still indicates the theme number, however, and the theme name remains in boldface type.

For Holidays, Seasons, and Events

136 **New Year's.** We have a tradition that we've done every year. I say, "There's an invisible line down the center of the studio. The old year is on one side, the new year on the other. Let's see what you do."

137 **Martin Luther King, Jr.'s birthday.** (1) "See Dr. King as one of many leaders, make him part of a long tradition." (2) "Do your version of the 'I Have a Dream' speech." (3) "Show your feelings for someone historical or someone you esteem."

138 **First day of spring.** June, a biology teacher in our group, gave us this order of events: (1) ground breaks, (2) frost melts, (3) grass pushes up, (4) crocuses grow, (5) sun comes out. To do this, each person in a group of five is one thing: One is the ground, one the frost, one the grass, etc.

139 **Easter.** The class suggested themes such as freedom, rebirth, and hope.

140 **July Fourth.** The theme is independence. "Add yourself, one at a time, to a group sculpture called 'Against Tyranny.' One person do a dance inspired by this sculpture."

141 **Autumn equinox.** What some students did: Jewel was leaves changing color. Gregory was the harvest moon (he got others to harvest corn, wheat, etc.). Maia was melancholy. Pauline was the chill of autumn and loss of summer.

142 **Yom Kippur.** Our theme on this day is atonement.

143 **Snow weather.** On a winter day like this the whole city is an improvisation class! It's the one time of the year when all people are conscious of the movements of their bodies. The snowy and icy streets make people look before they jump across curbs and while they are walking on the streets. Theme: "Do something for somebody you've seen trying to cope with these difficulties underfoot."

   At this time of year I teach all my pupils how to fall, starting with safe falling from a sitting position, then from a kneeling position, and finally from a standing position. Sally claimed that this training helped her when she fell with her baby in her arms. She managed to fall away from the side she was holding him on.

144 **Christmas.** One theme is peace on earth. We do "picture postcards"— one person arranges the others, then gives the card a spoken caption. We also have snowball fights.

145 **Birthdays, return from travels, etc.** We give (imaginary) gifts and/ or picture postcards (See Theme 93.)

146 **Weddings.** Before Lenore's wedding we created an aisle for her and had her practice walking between the (real!) white satin bands held by classmates.

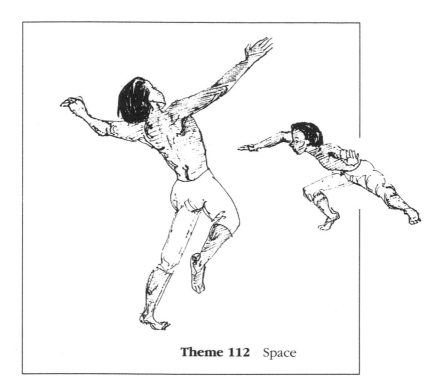

Theme 112 Space

Theme 116 Two groups

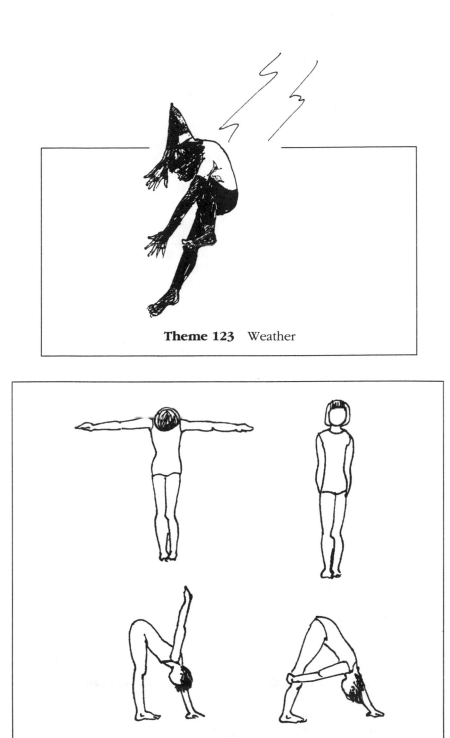

Theme 123   Weather

Theme 133   Introductions (TINA)

To Weld Individuals Into a Group

147   **"Add-a-Person: Make something new by adding you."** (Theme
      82) Two people hold hands and hold their position. A third person
      changes the design by entering the duo and moving so that the two
      must accommodate her. Then a fourth person is added, then a fifth,
      etc. (Excellent for feeling refreshed and "included"; helps change a
      static atmosphere.)

148   **Improvs for Ronna, who felt she just couldn't improvise:** "You're
      in a country whose language you do not speak. Convey your needs
      in movement."
          For example, "I'm hungry. Where can I eat? Things I want to eat."
      "I need to get to a certain place. What's the place like? How can I
      get there?" "I'd like to go to a lake or ocean to swim."
          "I'm hot (or cold)." "I'm tired. I'd like to go somewhere to lie down."
      "Do you have a cat? I have one at home."

149   **For Nancy, a newcomer:** "You be the sun in the center. Pat and
      Greg will start out from their separate, faraway, very cold climates,
      and be drawn to you by the power of your brilliance and heat." (I
      also gave this to Jonas, student Carol's child, who was with us. He
      loved being the sun around whom all moved.)

To Weld a Group Together After a Vacation, or Whenever They Seem to Need It

150   "Huddle yourself together. Now burst on the cymbal. Soft drumbeats
      bring you back into your huddle. Now when I play the cymbal, burst
      toward someone else in the group, reaching toward them, and then
      return to your huddle." Finally: "When you burst now, continue to
      move toward someone else in the group. We'll see what happens."

151   For three or four: "Move around freely. Freeze and close your eyes.
      Go to center of floor. Sink to floor. Find all hands around." (All six
      hands or all eight hands.)

152   For a larger group: (1) Theme 87: "Brew up a potion—all of you—and
      then use that brew in any way you need it, for yourself and with
      others." (2) "Make a statue, all together."

153   **"Apart and Together."** (See Theme 5.)

154   **Limitation**. "Hold hands all around. Move until you all stop together."

155   For two groups: **Rise and descend** at the same time, then at oppo-
      site times.

Improvisations for the Entire Group

156   **Choric** (Inspired by the Greek word *chorus*). If there is anyone who
      has some urgent "Personal Stuff," I ask that individual to do it while

the entire rest of the group forms a backdrop, responding to the improviser only as they are genuinely moved to do so. The group does not touch or interrelate; they just respond as background. We also do variations in which there is interaction between the improviser and the group.

157 **Clockwise, Counterclockwise**. I ask the group to make clusters in the four corners of the room. Then I call the names of two, three, or four in each corner and say, "Every time you walk, move clockwise." To the others in each corner I say, "The rest of you: Every time you walk, move counterclockwise. Now, everybody start to walk around, and please stay as much on the periphery of the room as possible instead of jamming into the center—even if you have to change the tempo or movement you're doing so as to keep your distance from the center. In the course of your walk you can stop to move with one or any number of others whom you meet, or you may just keep on walking by yourself." This continues until it stops naturally. (I say, "Continue until you all stop, and hold the end.") Most often, all do something together at the end.

158 **Kaleidoscope** (Theme 72): (For groups of four or five, simultaneously.) Ann takes a position. Ben fits in and around her. Cal fits in and around Ben. Don fits in and around Cal. Eve fits in and around Don. The moment Eve has fit in, Ann runs to another position and as swiftly as possible, Ben, Cal, Don, and Eve follow and fit in and around. This sequence continues for as long as all want to move.

First variation: Instead of running to fit in and around, each one moves to new position in whatever way he wishes, at whatever tempo.

Second variation: Ann takes a position that comes from an emotion, and all others run to her simultaneously, responding to that emotion. Then Ann runs to another place and takes an "emotional" position, and the group runs again in response.

When several groups do the basic sequence, the activity of all the groups can go on simultaneously until the time you have preplanned to hold the ending. For instance, you can all decide beforehand that each group will hold at the end of its fourth run. Any group that finishes its fourth run will stand (with the fifth person fitting in and around) and hold, waiting for the other groups to complete their fourth runs. This makes for interesting choreography, since all groups are moving at their own tempos.

159 **Tracks**. Everyone starts side by side at one end of the room. I say "What you see in front of you is your track. Stay within that track while you are going forward and back." I start the motion off by saying, "high and low." After they have done that for a long time, I say, "stop and go." After some time of that, I say, "fast and slow." Then, after a while, I say, "Now use all three: high and low, fast and slow, stop and go." Finally, I say, "Spot something that someone else

is doing in another track. Stay in your own track but copy that. The improv ends when all are doing the same thing."

160   Also excellent for entire group: All stand in a large circle and I say, "together and apart. Go until you all stop." (See Theme 5, "Apart and Together.")

161   **Group to percussion.** I say "Someone who wants to play the percussion, please do so." A player steps out of the group and stands with the percussion instruments. I say, "Please play a phrase for us, using any of the instruments you wish, or the drum alone, and keep repeating that phrase. The rest of you, move to the phrase."

Then, at various times during the playing, I'll say, "Hold!" to the movers and the player and suggest one of the following (done to the same phrase):

- Move on cymbals only.
- Some move on drum, some on cymbal.
- Keep moving, but relate to each other on the cymbal. Or, keep moving on the phrase, but relate to each other on a specific accent.
- Just do hand movements, on the African bells.
- Do not move at all, just on bells.
- Two go in front of the group while the group is background. The background people move on drum; the two in front move on cymbal.
- On the cymbal, decide whether you want to go deep down toward the floor or rise upward.
- On the cymbal, relate to two separate people. Or, on the two accents in that phrase, relate to one person on one accent and another person on the second accent.
- On the accent in the phrase, all relate to the percussion player. For the rest of the phrase you're on your own.
- Stamp on drum, clap hands on cymbal.
- Clap the entire phrase that the player is playing. Or, stamp the phrase. Or, alternate clapping a phrase and stamping a phrase. On the stamping you can move anywhere.
- Clap a phrase, then move on to the next phrase. Alternate clapping a phrase and moving a phrase.
- Decide whether you want to clap the phrase or stamp the phrase, and use the clapping and stamping as you wish: Do a whole string of one of them and then of the other, alternate, or combine.

Each person in the group who would like to be a player of the percussion gets a chance to do so.

Life as Theater

Here are two extraordinary themes for solos. I have timed them and they take from 10 to 15 minutes. They can be done in a very small class where each can take turns, given to one person per class throughout a semester, or one-to-one.

Both themes lend themselves to every category—artistic, emotional, imaginative, etc.—but the first is only for the most experienced improvisers; the second can be done with any beginner who has reached a state of trust. Both take the complete unwavering concentration of the onlookers.

162 **My life up to now.** This started as a joke, coming out of some group remarks after class that "we're moving out our lives" here in the studio. But each of my students has had a chance to improvise on this theme and it is amazing how an individual can select highlights and emotions from 20 or 30 years of living. Even more amazing is that the timing is almost exactly 15 minutes for everyone who has done it. I watch the clock without telling them, and then ask, when it is over, "How long do you think that took?" They never guess correctly.

163 **Child's play for adults.** I'm very proud of this concept, as it came organically from my observation of how students use props.

The teacher sets out as many props as possible—such as musical instruments, percussion, fabrics, and hoops—and invites the improviser to use in addition anything he sees around the studio or classroom (a bench, chair, pole, vase).

The theme is stated this way:

"This time is all to yourself as if nobody is around. You're just on your own to do whatever you wish with any of the things you choose to use. Again: We're not here. Take your time."

However these themes are used, improvisers always emerge from them with great refreshment, grateful for the opportunity to have had this personal time and attention.

Movement Improvisation

arouses	joy in moving freely
builds	confidence to move in front of and with others
communicates	meaning, thought, and mood
creates	a wider movement vocabulary
cultivates	clarity of image
develops	artistry and style
elicits	new approaches to thematic material
encourages	mind, emotions, and body to integrate
excites	discovery and adventurousness
explores	the widest variety of stimuli, the most diverse range of response
expresses	moods and emotions for which there are no words
extends	movement experience beyond technical exercise
frees	the body from restraint
furthers	awareness and sensitivity
gives	delight in the fresh and genuine
initiates	rhythmic phrasing and patterns
inspires	courage to experiment, boldness to innovate
permits	exposing socially unacceptable emotions in safety
promotes	respect for varied interpretations
releases	inhibitions and "noncreative" blocs
relieves	tension of everyday routine and stress
sharpens	conceptual thinking
spurs	the fanciful and imaginative
stimulates	interaction with others
strengthens	concentration and endurance
teaches	the discipline of artistry
translates	mood and concept into movement
uses	the body and imagination to the fullest
welds	a warm, trusting, and dynamic group

Index

About the Author

Lis Adams

Georgette Schneer has been teaching modern dance technique and theory for more than four decades. Her background includes interpretative dance with Bird Larson and Duncan dance with Irma Duncan as well as studies in the Humphrey, Wigman, and Graham pioneer idioms of modern dance. She has been director of her own studio since 1973.

Georgette, along with some of her experienced students, has led open workshops outside her studio since 1981. Known as The Roving Workshop, this seasoned group of improvisers travels to popularize the benefits of movement creativity. The group conducts presentations at professional conferences and in-service sessions for art, dance, drama, and music therapists.

Georgette is a member of the American Dance Guild and former director of the renowned Harlem Dance and Theater Company, where she helped youngsters shape dances from their lives. She received a fellowship from Rhode Island Creative Arts Center in 1983 to write about her teaching experiences. Georgette teaches and lives in New York City.